PRAISE FOR

"If you are tired of books full of pat answers, easy solutions, and sanitized language, look no further than *Shame*. Josh Roggie tosses aside all expectations of a Christian memoir and gives an honest, funny, and fresh take on how a Christian childhood informs one's life as an adult. In deconstructing the shallow religion of his youth, he finds a much deeper belief based in mystery and wonder. Do I agree with everything he says here? No. And that's a good thing. There is room for differences in Roggie's account, a quick-reading book that could as aptly be called *Grace*. It's a book seasoned with cussing and hard questions. An engaging, inspiring treat."

Eric Wilson
NY Times bestselling author of *Fireproof* and *Samson*

"Roggie's work is a hopeful, transparent, and timely read as our nation seeks to call out the unhealthy ways of toxic masculinity. Prepare to learn much from his vulnerability and be drawn into the loving embrace of a God who only squeezes us in closer in times of shame."

Meggie Lee Calvin
Bestselling author of *I Am My Own Sanctuary*

"What does it mean to grow up a Christian? Does faith change as we get older? If it does change, is that good or bad? Josh Roggie writes a very personal story that is both funny and heartbreaking as he explores these questions. His story stays true to a Christian's experience. It reflects what it's like to go from being told about God and what to believe, to making your faith your own."

Toby Morrell
Host of the "Bad Christian" podcast

"I found myself reliving so much of my past in this book by Josh. He has painted a beautiful picture here of what shame and guilt is at its worst, but more importantly how we can be freed from the bonds of it. It reminds me it's fine to fail at new things so long as I give myself permission to try new things. I loved every minute of this—and the soundtrack alone is worth the price of entry."

Seth Price
Host of the "Can I Say This in Church?" podcast

"Shame is a prison that keeps us hiding in plain sight from the very people around us who can help love us into freedom. In this beautifully-messy memoir, Josh Roggie shares his powerful true story of finding himself and letting his true voice be heard— curse words and all. As you read this heartbreaking and hopeful book, allow the courage and vulnerability poured out on these pages to infect your heart and nudge you out of the shadows and into the light of day."

Jason Elam
Host of the "Messy Spirituality" podcast

"Josh's book, *Shame,* is great! It's both vulnerable and funny, and should prevent any honest person of faith from being able to put it down. I hope every single Christian who has lived with guilt and shame reads this book. I believe it will go a long way toward helping them heal."

Matthew Distefano
Bestselling author of *Devoted As F*ck*

"*Shame* covers an abundance of topics from swearing to sex, body image to bullying, always keeping the focus on how shame can drive us away from others and from God rather than drawing us closer. Roggie doesn't hold back in talking about his own experiences and how that has shaped and molded him and his faith. It's an honest and sincere presentation of Josh's life that he invites the reader into—to listen, to learn, and to just simply share. And there's power in that kind of story, I think."

Josh Olds
lifeisstory.com

Copyright © 2019 by Josh Roggie.

First Edition

Cover design and layout by Rafael Polendo (polendo.net)

The following memoir reflects the author's present recollections of experiences over time. Some names and characteristics may have been changed, some events have been compressed, and some dialogue has been recreated.

ISBN 978-1-938480-53-9

This volume is printed on acid free paper and meets ANSI Z39.48 standards.

Printed in the United States of America

Published by Quoir
Orange, California

www.quoir.com

An Unconventional
Memoir

Josh Roggie

Table of Contents

Foreword

When I was growing up in the church, my pastor would take an extremely risky move by inviting members to "testify" to what God had done. Don't get me wrong, now that I am a pastor myself I find incredible value in shared stories and meeting each other as a community in our successes and failures. The problem and risk was found in those who often took that moment as an opportunity to awkwardly over-share their struggle of the week that would be better worked out in conversation with a friend rather than front and center during a Sunday morning service. Shortly thereafter, the discomfort would increase as a braggart seized the mic next and proceeded to wax poetic on how pious they were that week; or even better, share their opinion on the hot political issue of the day. It was brutal.

But, and this is a big "but" (ha!): On occasion, a pure testimony would occur, a moment where someone was able to communicate what God had done in their life with no hint of soapboxing. And it all seemed worth it. The testimony would be a perfect blend of vulnerability, humility, and desire for connection mixed well into a brief (key word) story informing the congregation on the journey their brother or sister in Christ had been on, and relayed how the community could better pray for or celebrate them. Those moments were beautiful; beautiful in the transcendent, aesthetic sense when Christ is encountered and the church as a true community is crystallized and validated, if only for a moment.

What Josh has done with this memoir/testimony/freestyle on his life and God falls into the category of pure testimony. He invites the reader to trek with him through a lighter conversation on swearing, the confusing world of theology while maturing into adulthood, and the heavy journey he and his wife have lived through infertility. Gracefully straddling the fence between genuine witness and over-sharing, the comedy and insights make every page, every story worth your time.

As a pastor, I accept the challenge put forth by William Willimon from his book, *Pastor,* to be a voracious reader so as to sharpen my own work as a wordsmith and communicator. This pulls me into a wide range of genres, including but not limited to theology, philosophy, or literature. The one genre that I perhaps appreciate most is the biography. I love a good biography, whether it be Chernow's *Grant,* McCullough's *Mornings on Horseback,* or Eberhard Bethge's magnificent tome on Bonhoeffer. The best biographies reveal a truth lost in the drudgery of day to day life—they shed light on how our lives tell a story.

Not everyone is going to live a life befitting a 1,000-page book set to be a *NY Times* bestseller decades later, but we can all tell a story like Josh's: a story that is raw and reflective and peace-seeking through the chaos of life and searching for beauty in the midst of tragedy, and loving better those that we care for. This book invites us to do just that, and for that reason it is well worth the read.

I have known Josh for coming on 20 years. I lived some of these stories with him and yet was surprised at how much about him I did not already know. I learned how I might better share my own story with others while reading this. I appreciate the honesty, humor, and insights offered throughout this book. Josh is the kind of member I would love to have at my church. The church is strengthened by shared stories because it is just that: a collection of shared stories.

The collection may include stories of creation, stories of redemption, or stories of a failed white rapper turned philosopher/author as we have here. It all belongs. Josh is quick to point out his lack of qualifications as a theologian, philosopher, etcetera; but where he *is* qualified is in the most important area: authenticity. This is his story, and in a move that is equal parts brave and vulnerable, he has shared it so that it may be our story as well.

I am honored to have been asked to write the introduction for this book, and I hope it will not be the last time that Josh finds himself slumming for a Foreword writer such as myself.

Here is to you, Reader, and your journey with Josh. What story does your life tell?

Rev. Matt Codd
Lead Pastor, *New Hope Community Church of the Nazarene*

Prologue

It was a Friday night in 2007. I couldn't tell you which Friday night, because I spent many of them the exact same way.

I had a job delivering hoagies and cheesesteaks during the lunch rush, which meant I didn't have to be to work until 11 a.m. and was off by 2:30 p.m. I would spend a relaxing afternoon playing Xbox or maybe taking a quick nap. My friends had various jobs, too, and were also in college classes (a move I had declined to make up to this point). Sometime around 7 p.m. or so, we would all meet up at Lazerquest. If the name doesn't give it away, you should know that this place was awesome. There was an arcade out front complete with typical games like Time Crisis, Cruisin' the World, and always something with zombies.

But the real action was the laser tag. They had a two-story arena with dual towers and mirrors to boot, to add an extra layer to the mayhem. Sure, sometimes there were birthday parties for 4th graders, but my nineteen-year-old friends and I had a blast.

We took it very seriously and would many times be dripping with sweat by the end of the match.

The night would be far from over, though. Next, we would all pile into our cars and drive across town to a specific Village Inn that we really loved. It didn't matter that there was another Village Inn literally right next door to Lazerquest. We had *our* Village Inn. There was this awesome manager named JB that would seat us where we requested. The table had a bronze plate screwed on it, labelling it "Booth 32", and we demanded that it be reserved for us every Friday night.

It's Village Inn. They don't do reservations. But the booth was always open and we rarely ever had to sit elsewhere, so you tell me. We ran the show there. We would do silly things like send "complimentary" pitchers of water to other tables if there were pretty girls sitting there. The waitress would point over to our table to let the prospective ladies know who would do such a kindness. We would sheepishly smile and turn appropriately red as we did know it was silly. Despite the cleverness on display, I can report a big fat zero in regard to the odds of getting phone numbers in return. So, single guys, don't bother. Ladies, you could probably get away with it. Guys are desperate even when they try to play cool.

We would also bring poker chips and cards and play Texas Hold 'em for a few hours. JB would play a hand with us here and there and would bring a pitcher of soda out to us when he would lose that hand. It suddenly occurs to me that we likely would have had more success with the pitcher of a refreshing beverage shtick had we sent over some fine Coca-Cola instead of water.

But the greatest part of the night was when I would order dessert. If it was a new waitress, she would always look at me with equal parts skepticism and disgust, with a hint of humor sprinkled in, and something I would like to think of as jealousy for my chutzpah. Which is ironically about the same amount of items in my custom dessert platter. Even better, the veteran waitresses knew it was coming because I was a regular. I called it the "Triple Decker". I would explain it to the waiter as something like this: "You start out with a nice slice of the NY style cheesecake as the base. Yes, you heard me, the base. Then I need a cut of the Triple Berry, 'cause it's the best pie Village Inn offers. Heat it up and put it directly on the cheesecake slice. Finally, let's get that a la mode, 'cause pie without cream is un-American."

If it sounds over the top, you're not wrong. But I kid you not, that was literally one of the things I talked about most at that stage in my life. I was genuinely excited about it and felt that I had created something. It became the story I told friends when they were back in town for Fall break from exotic places like Texas and Idaho. I went from AP English classes and varsity sports and graduating high school with a 3.8 GPA to opting out of college and living for these "wild" Friday nights.

Life was dull, to say the least. And we actually did this routinely, almost every single Friday night, for months on end. Teachers and adults and youth pastors tell you lots of things when you are a senior in high school. The world is your oyster and all that bullshit. And then, one night, you come to the conclusion that your greatest post-high school accomplishment is a special order of heart disease with a side of diabetes.

Add in that I had been raised a Christian and didn't really feel a single thing about faith, except the same dullness. I didn't bother to put much thought into my faith. The Christian faith was the way I was raised and was the way I would live, there was no question about it. Go to church, don't swear or drink, fall in love with girls (and only girls) as long as you don't touch them, don't touch yourself either, etc.

I had a plethora of sins that I was struggling with, and every day seemed like another lost battle in a never-ending war. I'll delve into these things some more, but at the top of the list was that classic example of lust and the isolation that often accompanies it. I thought I was all alone. Then, a revelation came into my life. It started with MySpace. Don't act like you're so young that you don't know what MySpace is, you're not kidding anyone. However, if you truly are too young to remember, it was *the* thing before Facebook, Instagram, Snapchat, or whatever the kids are using these days. The days of MySpace are long gone, but it was like having your own website, complete with your song of the week and custom background.

I had a friend and frequent Friday-night-hang buddy named Aaron. One night, I got a notification that he had written a new entry on his MySpace. I don't remember what the title was, probably something generic about a Bible verse he had recently read. Sounded kinda cheesy to be honest, but he was a friend and a good writer, so I took a chance to spend my next five minutes reading it. He started his post out with a reference to James 5:16 from the Bible:

"Therefore confess your sins to each other and pray for each other so that you may be healed. The prayer of a righteous person is powerful and effective."

My friend then went on to briefly but unambiguously describe his addiction to porn and his desire to stop looking at it. And he asked for prayer and accountability from anyone who would take the time to read his confession. He was writing from the computer in his parents' basement where he lived, but he didn't want to be alone any more.

———————

Let's be honest, that's kind of an awkward thing to talk about, particularly in the Christian world. You aren't supposed to look at porn, and if you do, you damn well better not talk about it. That's a good way to get kicked out of the twenty-somethings group or be asked to step down from your Sunday School teaching role. It doesn't matter what sins everyone else is struggling with behind closed doors, yours being known means that you are out.

Fortunately, my thoughts weren't quite that self-righteous from the get go. I didn't turn into Bible Man and tell him he was going to hell if he didn't stop this disgusting habit. However, my response was its own absurd degree of shallow. I could have thought about how I wasn't alone and somebody else, a good friend in fact, had struggles similar to my own. No, my thoughts were more along the lines of: "How the heck are you going to get a date now? Seriously, there is no way in hell a girl is going to date you after you just shared what your mind is like. They are going to think it is disgusting and so are you."

How many different ways was I being stupid and immature? It's clear that I didn't have many thoughts of ambition and goals outside of finding a girlfriend—that's never a good place to find yourself. And I thought it was likely more effective to pretend you are perfect and don't have any major problems rather than reach out for help on something so personal. I was ignorant.

Aaron's life story has gone quite well from there. I don't remember the exact time frame, but a couple years after this he started dating an awesome woman named Brittany. They started doing these great ministry activities together to grow and help others. I was even best man at their wedding and delivered a short little speech and everything. Since then, they have become frequent foster parents and board game aficionados. And they seem truly happy.

So, there was something to his idea. Clearly, a lot happened from his confession all the way to marriage, but I had to believe that bringing his struggles to the light had an effect. I would guess that it was still difficult, but something changed, too. It wasn't just him against the world in a dark basement. Porn was no longer a secret and he was no longer isolated.

Which brings something to my attention even as I write this. Why was it news to me that Aaron was dealing with this when I read that post? We were pretty good friends. Around this time, I would have considered him one of my best friends. We went so far as to buy a townhouse together when it was time for us to each move out of our parents' houses. I was the best man at his wedding, for God sakes! In my best man research, I found that one great potential speech would be to reference speaking the same length that the groom could last in love making. At which point, I would promptly end the speech with a mic drop. I *should* have done that instead of the nervous, incoherent mumblings I had improvised. To be fair, his parents likely appreciated reality more than the joke option, but it was still not my best work. If ever I get a chance to toast at his 20-year anniversary, I will be better prepared.

Despite having a relationship where I would eventually consider making a sex stamina joke at his wedding, I still didn't ever have the courage to talk with him about this addiction. We had deep conversations about God and philosophy and if pacifism is really a calling of Jesus. We would engage in heated debates about the rules of time travel and whether or not the Loch Ness monster could possibly exist (I'm not sure I'm a Nessie believer, but I refuse to accept that it is not even possible. And my logic is right.).

But we would never discuss anything personal such as the things we were truly struggling with. And certainly, never porn addiction. It's really not that hard of a puzzle to piece together. Whether it is explicitly stated or not, church people are taught not to share their darkest secrets. Premarital sex, extramarital affairs, lying, cheating, stealing, gluttony, drug addiction: there are some ugly, messy parts of our lives. Christians are supposed to be the saved ones who don't do those things anymore.

And yet, the Bible is pretty clear that everyone sins and falls short. Furthermore, bringing Jesus into your life doesn't make sin magically stop. Life change is supposed to happen with Jesus, but there are still shitty parts of our past and present and even our future. These are things that we feel shame about. It is an affront to God… right?

Shame is a weird thing. It's this feeling where we feel sorry about the things that we have done. And yet, it's not a constructive sorrow that we feel. Quite the opposite. It's usually more debilitating or scarring or identity-robbing. I will always be "a failure, an adulterer, filthy mouthed, a faithless and scrawny little kid with no self-confidence." I have been all of those things at one point or another. I don't want to be controlled by them anymore.

I had this idea to write a book about myself. I've got some funny stories, and some messy ones; a lot of the stories are both. As I started, I realized that many of these experiences had made me feel less than I am, distressed by embarrassment and guilt and yes, shame. But years after reading Aaron's blog post, I have been inspired to follow his example. I am no longer going to carry these burdens alone and I hope that modeling this will push you to do the same.

You'll notice that there are a lot of stories in here about growing up in a conservative Christian household and coming through the fray still a Christian. That's a part of who I am, but I promise I will not try to convince you to believe what I believe. I have no interest in that. I only aim to share who I am. That being said, you will likely get to know me more than you had ever planned. Thank you for taking the time to read the thoughts and events that left me at my lowest and would ultimately guide me through the stages of life that made me into who I am today.

All the Dirty Words

My parents were raised Mennonite. If you're not familiar with that term, many people like to assume it's similar to Amish. Turns out that the Amish were founded by Jakob Ammann in 1693 after he tried and failed to reform the Mennonite church of that day. So apparently the comparison holds some water. However, Mennonites remain their own distinct denomination with a wide scope of worship and doctrines across the globe.

Where I was raised in upstate New York, they were definitely very conservative, a culture somewhat to itself though not isolated to the culture around them, and not really into the frivolous things of life. Their doctrine included pacifism, baptism, communion, and specific gender roles in which women were expected to cover their heads. To this day, many of my relatives continue to live by these guidelines. I can't say I know all the ins and outs of their doctrine, but their stance on swearing is pretty easy to assume with no risk of making an ass out of you or me. I was raised in this for the first few years of my life.

I vaguely remember the first time I would use a vile, dirty word. I suspect my mom remembers it in no uncertain terms. When I was about five years old, I would ride the bus home. My school was a private Mennonite school that used the bus system from a local public school. Yeah, I rode the bus with all those public school hooligans. I saw and overheard a lot of things. Things like girls with low-cut shirts and filthy mouths and guys describing in more vivid language who they wanted to bone. Things I was curious about and likely to echo when I got home, apparently.

When I was five years old, I came home one day after school and asked my mom, "What does fuck mean?" As far as I can tell, I was legitimately curious. Maybe I had an inkling that this might be a bad word and I could "get away with it" by acting inquisitive. I was that type of kid, so it is definitely possible that I was trying to exploit a loophole to rock the boat. Whatever the case, I legitimately didn't know what it meant, so that part of the equation is accurate. But there's only one way to find out.

To say my mom was upset is a bit of an understatement. Her oldest little angel said THAT word. My mom wasn't one for corporal punishment, but there was no way she was going to let me walk away unscathed, either.

So no beatdown with a belt, just a good ol' fashioned taste test of an exquisite bar of soap. Yep, she washed my dirty mouth out with soap. That was something that was done back then when you said something inappropriate. Have you ever tasted soap? Not got it in your mouth a little in the shower. I'm talking tasted it because a bar of Ivory soap was sitting on your tongue like a Jolly Rancher.

It's fucking gross. I don't remember the flavor. All flavors of soap are gross. But I can forgive my mom for this if she forgives me for saying fuck again.

That would not be my only run in over foul language with "the law" that my parents yielded. When I was in middle school, I played soccer. At this point, I was going to the public school with those very same hooligans I mentioned from the school bus. They were the ones that taught me fun words that changed my diet to soap. Clearly, I wouldn't have ever heard these words otherwise; in all likelihood, my virgin ears would still be untainted to this day. We didn't watch many movies or television so I think my parents may actually have believed this way. But now I wasn't only attending a public school, I was playing sports.

I had never played soccer before, but it seemed like a really fun thing to do. This was the first time boys soccer was introduced at our school. It was exciting to be a part of something new with my friends, even if I had no experience or knowledge of technique. I was a scrawny, short kid whose mom wouldn't let him sign up for tackle football. Plus, I was really fast. Seemed like soccer would be my ticket to a better social standing.

My best friends went to another school nearby and they played football, but I was playing soccer. My mom wouldn't let me play football, because she was afraid I would get hurt. I would later talk her into letting me play in high school. The first day of tackling drills, I got hit squarely on the chin and with the help of a mirror could see sinews of my skin desperately trying to hold my face together. I only needed six stitches, but I guess there was some validity to her concerns. But in middle school, soccer was the only option I was allowed to entertain during the fall season.

This sounds like I regret soccer, like I hated it so much that I must have cursed out my coach or had a huge blow up with my parents. Wrong. Soccer is awesome. I loved every minute of it. It was so much fun. If you've never played it, then don't knock it. It's not for everyone, but it was one of the most redeeming parts of my middle school experience.

While on the team, I remember a conversation I had at my church with one of those football-playing best friends, Matt. My family had since left the Mennonite church and started attending a Nazarene church. If Mennonite is one step above Amish, then this church we were going to was one step above Mennonite on the conservative scale.

One time, we did a youth-led service for Sunday morning service and the 60 congregants who regularly attended. My friends and I picked out a song by 38th Parallel called "Higher Ground." They were this incredible Christian band with back and forth rap/rock vocals akin to Linkin Park. It's a travesty that they never blew up the way LP did. We picked the softest song 38th Parallel had, but it was still vetoed by the pastor. There were electric guitars in the background. Not heavy riffs or crazy solos or anything, mind you. Just that there were electric guitars at all was the problem. It was "too heavy." Instead, one of the absolute softest songs by DC Talk, titled "Red Letters." No "wild" guitars and loud drums to speak of.

While at this very same church one Sunday, I felt compelled to explain to Matt why I didn't play football. We were in the church's gym, hanging out after the service. Maybe I felt some shame around not being able to play football, or maybe I was just talking the way kids do without any real motivation. I told him, "I don't want to get my ass kicked." That was the reason I didn't play football.

He kinda looked at me in surprise, and I know I turned beet red with embarrassment. Or shame. Or whatever makes you turn red when you said something that might get you in trouble. I did what any self-respecting 12-year-old would do. I begged him not to tell anyone that I said "ass."

The funny part is that I would bet anything Matt was swearing sometimes, too. It's even funnier to say it that way. Like we were all secretly doing drugs or something. "I think he was probably on the swears. That kid is troubled."

But that's what it felt like. Like it was the end of the world if my parents found out. If I got caught, one could only wonder what fresh hell would rain down on me. I wouldn't eat soap ever again, honesty be damned.

It feels kinda silly doing a whole chapter on swearing. For most people, swearing is a non-issue. It's the communication equivalent of discussing the value of McDonald's. Should you eat it all the time? Hell no. But indulging every once in a while isn't going to hurt anything, and occasionally it could even be a real good time. That's my perspective anyway. If you want to eat McDonald's all the time, I won't judge you.

But for Christians it's a big deal. Or at least it used to be. I feel like it's becoming less of an issue. I know the biblical arguments about Paul saying not to use vile words or obscenities or crass jokes.[1] I also know the arguments that can be made for it about Paul calling his life shit before he found Jesus.

"Indeed I count everything as loss because of the surpassing worth of knowing Christ Jesus my Lord. For his sake I have suffered the loss of all things, and count them as REFUSE, in order that I may gain Christ." (Philippians 3:8, RSV, emphasis mine)

Other translations replace "refuse" with "garbage" (NIV), "rubbish" (NASB), "dung" (KJV) and so on. You won't exactly find the word "shit" in any Bible you pick up today, I would expect. However, the argument goes that shit would be the modern equivalent of the profane Greek word that he used, *skubalon*. I'm not a Greek scholar and won't pretend to be. But the argument is out there either way, for that and other verses. From where I'm sitting, it looks like the apostle Paul swore!

There are lots of things in the Bible that don't need to be taken literally. It's not that hard to figure out that some of it is clearly metaphorical. Ask any ultra-conservative Christian their thoughts on the Songs of Solomon, and they will stammer their way through an explanation about how it is about God's love for his people.

"Your stature is like that of the palm,
    and your breasts like clusters of fruit.
I said, 'I will climb the palm tree;
    I will take hold of its fruit.'"

(Songs of Solomon 7:7-8, NIV)

That sound like anything other than some solid foreplay to you? And yet, the Bible often gets treated like it is only a literal book designed for rule making.

---

1   Colossians 3:8, Ephesians 4:29, and Ephesians 5:4.

Another example comes to mind. For a while, I was into rap music and even wanted to pursue the art of being an emcee (more on this later). I wasn't into really good rap music, mind you. I wasn't allowed to listen to that stuff because of all the vile language, of course. But some of the songs used the word "fool" in them.

Seems pretty mild, really. There are a lot of things I could call someone that seem much worse. Things that would make you cringe. "Retarded" used to be a word we threw around no different than jerk or tool. It is rightly accepted nowadays that that word should not be said, because it is offensive to the mentally handicapped. Growing up in the 90's, I don't think I ever got in trouble for using it. It was no worse than telling someone they were being dumb. But fool was another case altogether. Because the Bible is very clear about it. Matthew 5:22 states, "And anyone who says, 'You fool!' will be in danger of the fire of hell."

That's pretty straightforward. It gets worse. That line is in red in the Bible, which means it came straight from the mouth of Jesus himself. I don't know about you, but if you care at all about the Bible, it seems like the red words should probably be considered the very most important. And yet, I don't think that's really what Jesus meant. He frequently talked in parables and metaphors and talked a damn lot about what was inside the heart and how to treat other people. He didn't seem too concerned with rules.

———

When I was in 9th grade, I would find new ways to hurt people without using swear words. My parents had made the decision to move the family from upstate New York to Colorado. I was pissed, to say the least. This wasn't exactly a family decision up for debate, but I put together an argument for why we should stay. My parents joke that I was always the lawyer of the family. I plead my case adamantly.

All my friends are here.

Our band, Addicted, is thriving. (Side note: You can't call it a band if you sing other bands' music together and play no instruments among four members. It's not any truer if you write dozens of songs, but only have the lyrics. Those are poems at best. And they were not good. R.I.P. Addicted.)

They have much better syrup in New York. I mean, do they even have maple trees in Colorado?

Really, those are the only points I can remember. They were tenuous at best. As you might imagine, we ended up moving to Colorado. So, I threw a fit of epic teenage proportions. I told my parents I hated them and they were being so selfish and didn't care about me at all. I told them when we got to Colorado, I would stay in my room all the time and would probably end up killing myself.

I was being entirely authentic, though obviously melodramatic. In my enraged state, I really thought that I would succumb to depression and want to kill myself. I don't think I said a single swear word *at* them or even in their presence. That was a line in my head that was "inappropriate" and I would never cross it, because… soap, right? Swearing would have been a sin. Instead, I told them that I hated them. For days on end, I reminded them that they might as well kill me now and save us all the grueling trip.

I was terrible. Swearing wouldn't have made those things any worse. The things I chose to say were cutting into their hearts without me using a single "bad word." I could have just quietly muttered that it was bullshit and walked to my room and never said anything on it again. That would have been a lot *less* offensive and cruel than the non-cursing words that I did use.

But I knew what I was doing. I *wanted* them to *know* the offense that I was feeling. I wanted them to hurt like I hurt.

———

Sometimes we feel shame because of the things that we do to other people. That's how I felt about the way I treated my parents for moving me to Colorado, all because I couldn't see how much better this move was going to make my life. Other times, I think we feel shame over the things we do only because of how we are treated after we do them. Are we internally ashamed over what we did or shamed by those around us?

When I was a junior in high school in Colorado, we had an assembly on the last day of school. It was a small private school, and there were about a hundred students in there. Near the end, the faculty opened up the stage for any student to come up and say what they had learned that year about life or God or whatever was on their mind.

It was a fine idea, I guess. But it was the last day of school, damnit! We just wanted to get out of the building and hit summer hard. I had visions of video games all night and the occasional pool parties where there would be girls in bikinis. And yet here we were, with an assembly bent on taking an eternity to end. Several students took their turn going up front, saying how they felt closer to God since dating so and so, or thanking all four of their best friends for helping them through the hard, indescribable times at a middle-class Christian private school, or whatever other bullshit was on their mind.

That's no disrespect to anyone who did speak that day. We were in high school, pretty much anything I would have had to say would have been drivel, and that's okay. It's high school. Somehow, after a handful of students, I ended up on stage alone holding a microphone. I had been sitting there in the pews (we met in a church sanctuary) and had something wriggling at the forefront of my mind. I had something that needed to come out. I was nervous. My palms were sweaty, knees weak, arms heavy. Ready to drop bombs. (There weren't enough Eminem references in my first draft).

I looked sheepishly down at my toes and cleared my throat, "I learned a lot this school year. It was a good year (pause for dramatic effect). You are all dismissed, have a great summer!"

Turns out, I did learn a lesson that day. It's hard for a dozen teachers to stop 100 students, especially on the last day of school. Everybody left the building.

That's a little bit of a badass moment for a small, Christian school. Everybody thought it was hilarious, and I felt really good about myself. I was getting pats on the back from the upperclassmen and cute girls were thanking me as I walked passed them in the hall.

My decision was completely validated until my English teacher caught me on my way out. She was an awesome woman nearing retirement and one of the first people to fervently encourage me to write. If you hate this book, I wouldn't *exactly* say it is her fault, but her efforts were definitely one of the earliest inspirations to stick with it. She was a wonderful teacher and did her best to direct me in learning the craft.

That day, however, encouragement was not on her mind. She gave me a very motherly look and said, "I'm very disappointed in what you did today." That's all she said. She didn't rip into me or try to punish me into next year. She just said that one statement that we all know are about the worst words anyone can say.

I wouldn't have felt bad at all about what I did. At the stage of life I am currently in, I again don't feel bad about it. It was hilarious. I remember it fondly as this rebellious thing I did that started a movement; even if that movement was a short-lived exodus that really only gave us an extra 20 minutes of summer.

Of course, just because I don't feel bad about it doesn't mean I was right. In reality, there's a strong argument for my teacher having the correct perspective. Truthfully, I don't think it was a big enough deal to be right or wrong and I'm guessing very few people in the room that day even remember it happening. I do know that I did feel bad because of the way I made Mrs. Powell feel. She was representative of how some others felt, too. Her disappointment left me feeling ashamed, even if briefly so.

Shame is a versatile feeling, with close cousins found in guilt and embarrassment. Shame is a response to something that is morally wrong or not up to standard for one's cultural or societal standards.[2] Though I know my mom didn't want me to carry shame through the years, she was using shame as a mechanism to teach me that swearing did not align with our culture's standards. When I cursed in front of my friend, I found myself feeling distressed at having done something morally wrong. It's true that I didn't want to get in trouble, but I specifically didn't want

---

2   I found this article by Neel Burton to be very helpful: https://www.psychologytoday.com/us/blog/hide-and-seek/201408/the-psychology-embarrassment-shame-and-guilt

to be exposed as being less than the expectations of my family. I felt that I failed the code.

Guilt is typically associated with feeling as if one has done something bad, rather than feeling as if they can be defined as bad. When my English teacher pulled me aside to correct me, she was not intending to shame me but her words were made to make me feel guilt for something that I previously thought was a good thing. While this feeling is distinct from shame, the realization of feeling guilt from hurting others can lead to feeling shame. For example, when I told my parents that I hated them. I followed all the "moral" rules that I understood, but when I saw that I hurt them I later felt guilt (for having done so) and shame (for being the type of person who would do such a thing).

Whereas shame is a responsive feeling towards one's moral status and guilt is tied to a feeling of a wrong action, embarrassment is tied to the image we want people to see when they look at us. When something happens that doesn't align with that image that we want to project, we feel embarrassment. It is not related to right or wrong. This is (one reason) why someone instinctively stops picking their nose when someone else catches them. They likely feel no shame about who they are as a person or true guilt for doing something that should be considered amoral, but they are briefly embarrassed to be thought of as "gross." However, there have been moments in my life where I felt so deeply embarrassed by my circumstances that it evolved into feeling ashamed as my self-image was at risk of being lowered.

At this point, I feel no guilt over swearing. For years, I thought it was sinful and would think that if I swore again I could go to hell. But I no longer believe words carry more weight than God's grace. Rather, I am more careful about what I am communicating and the intent behind that communication. I also feel no shame about this, as most people in my world have come to similar conclusions that swear words are not inherently hurtful and hurtful words are not always swear words. I do sometimes still feel embarrassment, such as when I may slip up and say a word that makes my parents uncomfortable (I may be an adult, but I'll still do my best to honor their rules), but that is a rarity and the feeling is fleeting and dissolves quickly. There is no long-lasting shame.

In many ways, I am prepared to feel embarrassment just by the release of this book. I am quite proud of it. But you, the Reader, are going to become acquainted with me in deeper and more uncomfortable ways than everyone save for my closest friends. I am going to reveal all of the different ways in which I have felt and experienced things that fall under the all-encompassing umbrella of feeling ashamed. And it turns out swearing was ultimately a small aspen in a forest of fucking Redwoods on the journey of addressing my shame.

When I Was A Shadow

I was a minor god at kickball. On the hallowed blacktop of Beaver River Central School, I defined the game for the next generation of ballers. By the time I was in fifth grade, I had a solid kick, a lightning fast sprint from base to base, and the quick-snap vertical to jump over any fast balls intended to get me out. *The Sandlot* was actually based on my life, they just switched it to baseball for a wider audience. I thought you could impress girls with kickball, but in hindsight that part never really panned out very well.

Turns out it also wasn't enough to be popular and not get your ass kicked by bigger kids. Once again, kickball just wasn't mainstream enough.

The best and worst times were during recess. We would all go play outside. I was actually relatively athletic, despite my small size. If we played kickball, I was golden. Not only was it fun, but I felt like a peer and not a victim. It was the other days that were ugly.

Recess sucked on the days where there wasn't a game to be had. I would find myself roaming the outskirts of the playground, typically alone since I didn't have any close friends at school. I have to admit, I don't remember any specific traumatizing moments. It's more like a montage sequence, but instead of the hero pumping iron he frequently finds himself the test subject of one of his "buddies" trying out new wrestling moves on him without his consent.

I have no idea how many times they would usher me over and use a wide range of WWE moves on me, including the "Stone Cold Stunner." If you're unsure of what that is, the Internet will tell you that it's a move in which you hold the opponent's jaw on your shoulder in an overhead face lock and then drop to the ground in a sitting position so their jaw takes the brunt of the impact on your shoulder. I will tell you that it apparently is a move in which I get my ass whooped in a variety of ways.

I would plead for them to stop, to give me a break today, to leave me alone for once, to start up a game of football instead; and they would go ahead and pummel me anyway. I also remember hitting my head more than a few times so maybe the occasional concussion eased the pain, or at least the memory. I didn't know what to do to stop it. All I could do was take it and try to minimize the damage done, whether through submission or humor.

———

Growing up, I was the little guy. It was bound to happen. My dad clocks in at about 5'7", and my mom hovers around 5' flat. If you look at my uncles, I think *one* of them *might* hit six feet. Most all of my cousins are smaller, too. And if they do have any size, they got it from the other half of their genes and not the half that I share.

Not that all small kids get bullied, but it is a stacking of the deck to begin with. I was a bit of a mama's boy in a family that held some scars from domestic abuse—which meant no fighting in the house. I had a younger brother, but my mother was adamant that we wouldn't ever rough each other up. Add in that I was embarrassed by the way I looked and was shy and meek as a method of camouflage to blend in and I never really learned how to stand up for myself.

Suffice to say, I never really had a chance to be a towering force roaming the streets of school. I tried everything I could to disappear in the crowd and not be noticed. That's tough to do when you're in a small school in a small town. There's not much to hide behind. So, I was bullied. For a long time, by several different people.

I don't think my parents knew about it. There weren't usually visible signs of bullying on me like cuts or anything. Most of my bruises were covered by clothes. The "beatings" I took were often psychological as much as they were physical. Many of my memories of the scuffles are more me pleading for them to leave me alone rather than lasting injuries. But even if my parents had seen the signs, I guarantee that I would have lied about it anyway.

I definitely never told them a single word about the whole thing. I wanted to be self-sufficient and it seemed as if they had enough troubles of their own. Around this time, my parents had some marital problems that led to a lot of arguing. Thankfully they were able to work through those issues a long time ago, but overhearing it as a child from the next room over made it feel eternal. My disposition is very much a peacemaker—I'm an enneagram 9 for any personality test nerds out there. It likely stems to some degree from these circumstances.

Sometimes, I would leave my bed and go to where they were, trying to convince them to stop arguing. Other times, I would lie awake for hours hearing their muffled words through my bedroom door. I was the oldest child in the house, and if anyone was getting us kids through this, it was me. That was how I saw it, anyway. I put all the weight on my shoulders, whether or not my siblings expected me to. I don't know if they even really remember this stuff since they were younger than me. At any rate, mum's the word.

I also didn't want anyone to know, because getting bullied is extremely embarrassing. People act so surprised when a victim says they were ashamed to tell someone. But most of the time, a response is likely to be an answer for what you are doing wrong that is causing the bullying. It's probably not intended that way, but what does it sound like when I say, "You need to do this, this, and this." It may even be right advice, but the wrong tone can make it sound like chastisement.

Not to mention what might happen if my parents went to the school and they tried fixing it that way. I'd probably get bullied more for running to mommy and daddy and a teacher than for my big teeth and skinny body that was already inspiring the physical and verbal torment. It seemed like it would only make things worse if my parents were in the know on it.

At its core, the feelings of isolation were key to the success of the people bullying me. I needed to know that I wasn't alone, but everything about my experience suggested to me that it would be best if I didn't seek out help. Had I found help, it likely would have ended sooner and hopefully would have left less scars. Instead, it was a common thread running through my earliest years all the way through middle school and would even occasionally provide flashbacks in early adulthood.

———————————

As far as I can recall, the bullying started when I went to a Mennonite school for my elementary years. One of the main principles of Mennonite beliefs is that of pacifism. This is really an important tenet in all of Christian tradition, but one that tends to be forgotten and disposed of by Evangelical American Christianity. If you've never thought about it, but consider yourself a Christian, then now is a time to start studying it. It's a complex topic and Jesus talked a lot about it, so you can't just gloss over and ignore it. An excellent starting point for research is "Fight: A Christian Case for Non-violence" by Preston Sprinkle.

For our purposes, the simplest definition of pacifism will be to live a non-violent lifestyle where one does everything they can to harm no others.

At that time, the people I went to school with were Mennonites. Most of my church experience growing up was Mennonite. My cousins are almost all Mennonite. So, it's anybody's guess how I managed to find myself getting bullied in this environment. I am getting shoved around and pushed and pinched by a bunch of pacifists!

In truth, it's really not that hard to figure out. At the end of the day, boys are assholes. I'm sure there is proof that the same can be said of girls, but my worst hurts were at the hands of boys in those days. With boys, it's hard to discern the difference between bullying and just roughhousing, especially at that age. I guess there probably isn't a clear definition. Maybe once the roughhousing seems to target a specific person and stretches beyond that person's ability to endure it.

I was the specific person, for sure. And I constantly felt anxiety around if it would happen again today. I even remember seeing somebody else get bullied, and then a couple days later, that dude that was the victim was bullying me instead. He was passing on the hurt to the next person a rung below him. I didn't pass it on; the reign of violence ended with me. I don't think I was brave, I think I was weak. Or maybe scared.

Whatever the case, I didn't take the bullying upon myself because of my pacifist beliefs. Kids don't think that way. Even if I had believed in that methodology, there are different forms of non-violence, such as: justified war pacifism (certain situations require violence to resolve), self-defense (pacifist except when in self-defense of myself or other people in need), etc.

That's a simple way to put it and falls short of the weight and complexity of those concepts. But there were arguments that meant that I could have defended myself even if I did want to be a pacifist. This is not an argument for or against pacifism. It's just a story of a kid who got beat up a lot.

———

I was a kid who got beat up by Mennonites. I vividly remember being scratched, punched on the legs, bitten, etc. Again, it's not just roughhousing when the same people are doing it to me repeatedly, and I'm not retaliating in any way.

It only got worse from there. For unrelated reasons, I went to a public school when I was in the 4th grade. I went from being the small, defenseless kid at a tiny Mennonite school to being a small, defenseless kid at a bigger public school. It was a defining moment, the time where I needed to set my reputation. You've seen the movies. Find the biggest, baddest dude on the first day of prison and beat his ass in front of everyone to set your rep. I'm no expert on prison, but I don't know if it works that way. It *might* have worked in the 4th grade.

Either way, I didn't do it. I don't clearly remember when the bullying started again, but it seemed pretty immediate. Some of the kids bullying me on the school bus (remember it was the same bus system for both schools) were now my classmates who I saw all day. And new people joined in. I was picked on for wearing pants that were "high waters," meaning cut too short on the legs. They were holdovers from the Mennonite school uniform. So, I finally talked my parents into buying me a couple baggy pants, and then got made fun of because they were K-Mart brand.

My two front teeth were bigger than most and stuck out some, so I got called "Bucktooth" a lot. That one stung for a real long time. My parents wanted to give me braces to correct my overbite, but I gave them so much pushback, because it would be the pants all over again. I knew how to hear "Bucktooth," but I didn't want to be "Tinsel Teeth" next. I got braces eventually, and I'm glad I did, but I literally fought them for weeks on end with tears streaming down my cheeks.

The older I got, the more cruel it became. Once you get to the age of changing clothes in the locker room for gym class, you're in deep shit. The thin veil of security found in clothing is no longer promised. These times made the wrestling moves from recess seem like a cake walk. They would snap towels at me, especially trying to hit me when I was naked. I would hurriedly try to put my clothes on my wet body because there was no time to dry off, sometimes still so wet that my hair would freeze outside while waiting for the bus. If I didn't get out in time, a few of them would gang up on me and trap me in a corner and try to drag me to a toilet for a swirly.

Have you ever been dragged by a small crowd of guys stronger than you to a toilet so they can dunk your head in the bowl and flush the water down on you? I pray to God you can say no, because it was nightmare-inducing. The whole time they are hooting and hollering and laughing it up while you are literally begging them to stop. They keep talking about how they can't wait to give you a swirly. Maybe someone even left a dump in there for you to catch on its way down. I truly hope you have never experienced this—I have felt that fear.

I pushed back and struggled with everything I had. There was no way in hell I was going to live through a swirly. If I didn't suffocate, I knew I would drown in embarrassment when my classmates next saw me. I must have resisted enough during those times, because I never had the experience of them actually getting me into the toilet. Or maybe the guys were just loud mouth idiots and not strong enough to lift me.

At any rate, I'm thankful to never fully experience that. But it was still terrifying, never knowing if they were going to come at me again. Add in some other typical tactics, like wedgies and getting shoved into lockers, and it was a nightmare pretty much across the board. This lasted almost all the way through 7th grade. This was not one time, but literally dozens.

There was another time when we went on our school field trip at the end of the year. It was always somewhere pretty cool, like a trip to a water park or a planetarium. This particular year, the trip was to a local campground with a creek, open fields to play in, and an overabundance of hotdogs. Doesn't sound too exciting, but it was upstate NY and there wasn't exactly a lot of options and SHUT UP! It was awesome.

Until at one point some friends (by friends I mean that gray area where you see a lot of overlap with the people you spend time with and the people who bully you) and I got the bright idea to start throwing rocks at each other. I mean, throwing them the way you would throw a baseball: wind up and let it rip. And not even pebbles, but nice, long rocks that are thin and smooth. These are the type you use to skip rocks on the water. We found the flat sides made it so they could slice through the air in unexpected trajectories.

And one sliced through my ear. It didn't cut if off by any means, but it was a nice gash. My so-called friends begged and begged me to tell the teachers that I fell. This was my one chance to bust the same people that pushed me around and tried WWE moves on me, but instead I told a very unconvincing lie. Convincing enough, I guess. Nobody ever pushed me on it. Maybe the teachers looked at me the way someone might look at a battered spouse with a black eye after they say they just fell down the stairs. I wasn't bullied, I just fell a little.

This whole time that I was being bullied was in the 90's. It was before any of my peers had cell phones and we didn't have access to internet outside of school research projects. Even at home, we only had dial up internet which was so slow that it was nearly unusable. I was fortunate in this way, because it meant that my tormenters had no access to continue the agony when I wasn't at school. Times are different these days.

It wasn't until 2014 that there was even a uniform definition for bullying on the federal level. The Center for Disease Control and Department of Education pieced together an overarching definition of unwanted aggressive behavior, observed or perceived power imbalance, and repetition of behaviors or high likelihood of repetition.[1] These definitions allow for various modes and types of bullying despite changing technology. And the stats of those affected are staggering:

- The 2017 School Crime Supplement (National Center for Education Statistics and Bureau of Justice) indicates that, nationwide, about 20% of students ages 12-18 experienced bullying.

- The same study indicates that among students ages 12-18 who reported being bullied at school during the school year, 15% were bullied online or by text.

- About 49% of children in grades 4–12 reported being bullied by other students at school at least once during the past month.

- The following percentages of middle school students had experienced these various types of bullying: name calling (44.2 %); teasing (43.3 %); spreading rumors or lies (36.3%); pushing or shoving (32.4%); hitting, slapping, or kicking (29.2%); leaving out (28.5%); threatening

---

1   This definition and the following statistics can be found at https://www.stopbullying.gov/media/facts/index.html#stats.

(27.4%); stealing belongings (27.3%); sexual comments or gestures (23.7%); e-mail or blogging (9.9%).[2]

- Cyber Bullying happens across all mediums of technology including social media, text messages, online video gaming, etc.

These numbers can both be alarming and disconcerting, but I see a silver lining in there, as well. We are not alone. If you are being bullied, you are not the only one. It's not only children, but adults also experience bullying and there's no shame in that. Know that you will not be treated this way forever. There are ways out of this. There are numerous resources out there available to you to know what to do next if you are being bullied or if you are concerned that someone else may be a victim. You can find a phenomenal starting point at the website: https://www.stopbullying.gov.

———

I did not have these resources growing up. I falsely perceived that I would need to resolve this on my own. It was causing all sorts of insecurities in me. I had big teeth and a scrawny body and was weak. I dressed weird and talked weird (since I didn't regularly swear). I won't feign manliness; this all hurt deeply. I was very adamant that I wouldn't cry when being bullied and that effort continued when I was at home by myself. I still cried at times, but I felt shame even when I was alone because I

2   Bradshaw, C.P., Sawyer, A.L., and O'Brennan, L.M. (2007). "Bullying and Peer Victimization at School: Perceptual Differences Between Students and School Staff." *School Psychology Review*, 36(3), 361-382.

thought this meant I wasn't a man. I eventually learned that this was all wrong.

I started to figure out more of who I was around the end of 7th grade, the time when most kids start to figure some of that stuff out. I bleached my hair blonde (it was the late 90's, it was actually cool then). I used hair gel to make it spike up every which way. I wore these obnoxious parachute pants that were blue-tinted camouflage. And I truly didn't give a fuck what anybody thought for the first time in my life.

And the bullying stopped. I'm not sure I outright caused it to stop, but it did either way. And a couple other weird things happened through this time. I was more respected by my classmates and participated in some extracurricular activities. I didn't have a girlfriend, but they started paying more attention to me. But it wasn't all good things. Another thing I remember is that I started to pick on and make fun of other people.

There's no excuse. I may have been bullied, but it doesn't give me permission to make fun of others. I never physically picked on people (see the above if you need to know why not), but I definitely joked on people. I pride myself in being quick-witted and I certainly used my super powers for evil at times.

I remember a specific boy in our class who was super awkward and dressed really weird. I don't know if he was special needs or not, but I would say there is a reasonable chance that he was and was just socially capable enough to be in the standard classrooms. Never bully anyone, but especially not a special needs peer. I have no idea what I said or if it was something that he even got wind of. It doesn't really matter. I do know a friend and I were definitely mocking him. It was a terrible thing to do. I remember my teacher lecturing me after class on why it was wrong, and the flashbacks I had of getting picked on more than solidified why I would be leaving this kid alone from now on.

I would crack jokes and have some good laughs, but I tried to never again contribute to any bullying. I hope that I succeeded in that and didn't contribute to some other kid's bully chapter in their life story. Wouldn't that be some terrible irony?

8th grade was a good year for me. My braces were taken off and I definitely felt some more confidence from that. I no longer felt the need to cover my mouth when I talked in class and I would raise my hand instead of only speaking when the teacher made me. I was also starting to grow a little. I never would be tall, but I was becoming more athletic in build and was a solid basketball and soccer player. I started becoming actual friends with some of the athletes in my class. They picked on me some, too, but it was more in the way all teammates take jabs at each other. I would verbally dish it back some and we would all laugh.

The talk of swirlies and Stone Cold Stunners all but stopped. I wasn't one of the cool kids, but I hung out with some of them, so I was part of the gang. Unfortunately, the bullying probably trickled down to someone else, but I wasn't a part of it. I would eventually run into other problems, like girl problems, but bullying became primarily a thing of the past.

———

The key was to stop giving a shit what other people thought about me. Sometimes that can be a bad thing. It's okay to care for your reputation, and it's a good thing to let people close enough to you that you value their opinion. For me, no longer caring was exactly what I needed. I stopped worrying so much about everyone else's opinions and started to have a little confidence.

But I found my escape through vulnerability, which is the answer to this problem. Vulnerability is what it takes to talk to a leader or peer about the ways we are being hurt. Vulnerability is what it takes to be yourself and dye your hair and wear whatever obnoxious clothes you genuinely like. Vulnerability is what will make someone see you as a person and not an object for their aggression. It may not always create an immediate solution, but it will open your eyes to who you are and you will find that being the victim is not what you were designed for. And people around you will sense this, too.

Granted, I overcorrected and decided for a long time that I wouldn't make myself vulnerable in front of anyone. *Why give someone enough power to let them speak to your identity?* I chose to be the only one who could define my identity. And that would cause a whole slew of other problems. But I needed to see the value in being vulnerable with myself before I could understand what it meant to be vulnerable in front of others.

I I I

Holy Shit

"The Restless" by The Matches

There are a lot of childhood memories driven by the scars of shame and disappointment. If it were an art form, I feel somewhere along the way as if I have become an expert at living absolute masterpieces. For a while, I thought I wanted to be a rapper. In case you didn't notice, you're reading a book by me rather than listening to a dope track with sick flows over bumpin' bass. I guess things don't always go the way we think they will and, many times, that seems to be when shame abounds through its ugly cousin: embarrassment.

I remember my first semi-sorta girlfriend in middle school giving me her phone number as we went separate ways from church camp. I'm not exaggerating when I say I lost that little slip of paper not five minutes later. I didn't have a cellphone to just punch it in then, so it was written on a note that fell out of my pocket at some point.

More importantly, I didn't give up my super awesome bucket hat that I wore inside out. She desperately wanted to keep it as a way of remembering me. A token of our liking each other (love is such a strong word for middle schoolers to be throwing around). I said no. It's probably fair to say that this was not true love. I felt pretty bad about the whole ordeal. It seemed like a real douchebag thing to do, even though losing the number was a genuine accident.

I felt embarrassed that this could have happened to me, and I also felt guilt as I hoped that this young lady didn't think I never intended to call her. I absolutely did like her, even if it was never likely to have a lifelong impact. This was uncomfortable, but there's certainly another level. If there is one thing that is potentially more embarrassing and shaming than anything else, it's the moments of bodily function mishaps and bathroom necessities.

———

When I was about eleven or twelve years old, I won a pair of tickets to a Christian music festival. It was called Kingdom Bound in Darien Lake, NY. It's a music festival at a Six Flags, which is a massive theme park complete with roller coasters and way too much fried food. So even if the bands suck, it's a win. But they didn't, not by a long shot. It was essentially a dream lineup for adolescent me.

Relient K, John Reuben, Skillet, Grits, and DC TALK!!! If you want a brief lesson in late 90's Christian music, then start the list here. If you want to maintain your sanity then I might recommend you continue reading. Some of that music did not age well. That's just what I was into then. Some of it has since lost my interest, but at the time it made me feel as if Christian music could be as good as secular stuff.

In a weird turn of events, I didn't really have a way to get to this music festival. I had won these tickets on my favorite radio station. My parents were not able to attend, so I was bringing one of my best friends with me. But even in upstate New York, two 12-year-olds obviously weren't getting away with driving a few hours from home. Somehow, my parents got hooked up with another local church and we just jumped in and rode with them.

In hindsight, this was a very bizarre circumstance. This was not a church we attended and I don't believe it was from within our denomination. Meaning that I'm not sure we even knew anyone at the church. My mom had called around to the local churches to see who was sending a group of teens and may have a couple open seats in their bus. I doubt there was much of a vetting process outside of this very simple criteria. I guess it's lucky this is an embarrassing bodily fluids chapter and not an "accidentally stumbled into a cult" chapter.

Long story short, it was profusely hot that summer. The concert was in the middle of July, and I didn't have any parents telling me what to do. That seemed amazing, but it turns out I was ill-prepared. Sometimes you need an adult around, just to tell you to drink a cold glass of water instead of another Mountain Dew.

I'm sure the food was far from gourmet, too. One night, the group we were with had a huge pot of meaty spaghetti sauce and was ladling it onto English muffins and topping it off with mozzarella. It was awesome. It was also indicative of the nutrition levels the week held. As far as memory serves me, I didn't eat a single vegetable the entire week. I don't remember what exactly was on the menu, but we were spending our time exclusively at a theme park and a campground, so you do the math.

The lines for the rides were ridiculously long, too. It was this huge event and it was Six Flags, so every ride had waits over an hour-long.. We stood in line for a couple hours to go on the Superman Ride of Steel roller coaster, which was one of the highlight attractions of the park. The park attendants occasionally pulled out a hose and used their thumbs as makeshift sprinkler heads and sprayed everyone in line. And there was rejoicing by all.

So, I'm standing in line somewhere in the park, and it's hot, and we are under the sun for hours on end. Relief is scarce and water more so. The food is leading me to repeatedly…break wind. I'm doing it as politely and quietly as possible. It would be embarrassing if someone around me heard it. I'm basically doing everything I can to not draw attention to myself. It seems to be working, although I notice that some of these farts are getting increasingly uncomfortable. I come to the realization that I should probably find a bathroom soon. Probably right after this awesome ride, in fact.

I start to let out another one and come to realize that I might be in trouble… have you ever seen the Ben Stiller movie *Along Came Polly*? There's a part where Ben Stiller and Philip Seymour Hoffman (R.I.P.) are at a party, and Hoffman suddenly runs up to Stiller and says we have to go *right* now. He goes on to explain that he has sharted, which is when you think you're going to fart and a little shit comes out.

I was an independent middle schooler who didn't need adult supervision because I was a man, damnit! And in the middle of Six Flags, I definitely had just sharted myself. Not just a little bit, either. It could only be described as diarrhetic. Fortunately, there was no trace of evidence *around me* (other than a stench, I'm sure). Look, I know it's crude and disgusting and all those other things. I'm not exactly bragging here. I was so embarrassed by it that I have literally only told a handful of people this story.

The only commentary I can add is that I think I owe my friend big time (Bryan McGillvray, you are a gentleman and a scholar). That was, without a doubt, the most embarrassing moment of my life up to that point, and I don't think a single word was ever muttered of it. He didn't even make fun of me then, let alone spill the beans when we got home. He didn't need to. I already felt so much shame around it, because it was such a disgusting, childish thing to have happen. We grabbed an adult chaperone (who was essentially a complete stranger since we didn't know anyone from this church) and he graciously bought me a pair of swimming trunks as I threw away the tainted remains. And I literally never told this story again. "I sharted" isn't exactly the best icebreaker in most circles.

Embarrassment seems to know no boundaries of age or timing. When I was in high school, I talked myself onto a road trip with a couple friends. A married couple and a few of the teens were going to visit their former youth pastor. The drive from Colorado to Washington runs something like 17 hours, and they had an extra seat in the van.

We need to take a moment to set the stage a little here. First off, I absolutely did not invite myself on this trip—I was asked to tag along because I was homeschooled and thus my schedule was open. I was good friends with twins Matt and Terrance and it just made sense that we would visit their former youth pastor together, even though I had never met him before. This happens to be the very same Matt Codd who wrote the foreword to this book. He told a lot of truth in that opening, but don't bother asking him about this trip. He will say that he clearly remembers me inviting myself, which I assure you is an outright lie.

Matt and Terrance were two years older than me and, being twins, looked very similar to each other. They were about 6'4" and 140 pounds soaking wet. They seemed to have an impenetrable confidence despite their goofiness, and their humor and laughter knew no bounds. They were not mean people, but their brand of building kinship was definitely everyone in the group laughing at each other and cutting up. Long story short, they were some bony-ass troublemakers, but great friends.

All that to say, it was just a bonus that the only other teen on the trip was a girl named Lisa, who I happened to have a nearly debilitating crush on. Not enough to do something crazy like invite myself on a road trip across half the country, of course, but it was certainly a crush of notable levels.

The adults leading the way had a toddler with them, and mom was pregnant again. They were nice people and personally invited me along the week before venturing out. Why wouldn't you last minute invite a teenager you have known for six months on a 17-hour road trip to visit a youth pastor he has never met? I don't see a need for further speculation about the reasoning behind my presence. It all seemed like a golden opportunity to see somewhere new, create new memories, and confess my absolutely genuine and not-at-all exaggerated undying love. As I said, it was a long trip. A lot could happen, right? And damn, did it ever.

My memories of the outgoing trip to Washington really only include snippets of a visceral nightmare. It was summer time and there were seven of us crammed in a van. With all the heat, along with the high of being on a road trip, I didn't pace myself very well on the beverages. The last story was a matter of dehydration, but there would not be a repeat scenario. I have no idea how much I drank or even what I had gulped down. All I know is, an hour or two passes since our last stop, and I have to go to the bathroom to point of nearly bursting. Look outside and see that we are in the middle of Wyoming with no bathrooms in sight.

Seems like a fairly run of the mill story so far, right? Wrong. For whatever unclear reason, we don't at any point pull over so I can just take a leak on the side of the road. I don't have an answer for that. I guess maybe I was too timid to make demands about what the state of the van was about to become. And obviously, with the toddler, pregnant mom, and girl crush in the car, an empty bottle was not a viable solution.

When running from North to South, a straight line through Wyoming is approximately 276 miles long. We were in the car for about 4 hours and 15 minutes in the state of Wyoming. The sudden urge to pee had started in the first hour of this leg of the trip. Do you know how many rest stops there are on the highway in Wyoming? I didn't count, but I feel confident in saying that over those 276 miles there are about maybe three *fucking* bathrooms!

So that's the pickle I found myself in. And it gets better. At this point, I am sitting between Lisa and Terrance in the back of the van. Why in the hell did I have to be sitting next to anybody, let alone her? The embarrassment of sitting next to the girl is obvious. I am not only in a lot of discomfort, but I am at this point visibly sweating. And not "it's seasonally warm, I may need to move to the shade" sweating. Nothing short of extreme hikes has since caused me to sweat so badly. Have you ever smelled a high school freshman who has clearly sweat all the way through his less than adequate deodorant? I'm sure it wasn't roses everyone was catching a whiff of.

To top it off, Terrance did what any good friend would do: he started poking me in the kidneys. Not tapping me or mimicking a joke, but forcefully pushing his bony six-inch finger into my bladder as hard as he could. I had no hope of stopping his prodding. Any loss of focus on keeping the dam closed would have been the end. I had one bathroom mishap at a theme park, there was no way in hell there would be a repeat of any sort, especially not in front of a girl that I was convinced I would likely someday marry.

There were a lot of other embarrassing moments on that trip, and not all of them were mine. Fortunately, I did manage to summon superhero degrees of willpower and managed to not piss myself in the middle of Wyoming. But that girl and I never did date. I think that can probably be traced back to this moment where I was literally sweating urine out of my pores.

Contrary to my own assumptions, bodily mishaps don't end when you become an adult. When I was about 20 years old, I finally got my first grown up job. I was a custodian at Focus on the Family—yes, *that* Focus on the Family. There's tons of commentary that I could add here. I'll actually restrain. Despite my "unquestionably liberal leanings" at this stage in life, I was quite conservative at the time. You could maybe even argue that around this time was when my so-called liberal ideology started to develop. Causation might be a stretch, but there is certainly correlation. So congrats, James Dobson, your organization started my sad and disturbing descent into… progressivism.

I was there for three years, and neither hated it nor loved it. If you ever wanted to know more, you could just ask me. But for now, let's leave it at Focus on the Family being a very flawed place that manages to also do some good things—you could probably describe a lot of places that way. I got to know some salt of the earth people along the way. It's also the first time anyone had ever told me about universalism, which is a doctrinal theory that all humans will eventually be saved by God and none will be condemned to hell. I was introduced to that by a co-worker and certainly not any "official" material the organization provided. It was refreshing to see people with wide ranging thoughts still fall under the umbrella of Christianity.

One night, we were all at our lunch break. I was a nighttime custodian, so "lunch break" was actually a late dinner that was around 8 p.m. I felt noticeably sick that night, but for some reason decided I was going to rough it and get through this. I was raised in that "keep your nose to the grindstone through everything" sort of way, so I probably didn't want to take time off, even if it was paid. That's a great perspective, but I'd recommend using sick time when you're sick. I was practically quarantined, as all my coworkers intentionally sat in the other corners of the room. Near the end of break, I started to feel everything in my stomach lurching.

I made a run for the bathroom, though it was hardly running. I made a split-second decision to run right past a trash can in the room and head out into the hall. Get to the bathroom and everything will be okay. It would be embarrassing to throw up in a trash can in front of everyone. Good plan, except no more than two steps out of the break room, I started to gag.

I'll spare the gory details for my sympathetic vomiters out there, but my attempt to stop it from happening by holding my hand to my mouth definitely didn't work. I fell to my knees like the movie *Platoon* and started throwing up on the hallway carpet. The security camera in the corner of the doorway caught the whole thing.

The best part of this episode: who do you call in a public place when something needs to be cleaned? You guessed it, the janitors. So, they made me clean it up myself; those cold, heartless bastards at Focus on the Family. James Dobson himself stood over me and threatened my job when I took too long. He smirked at my sickness and embarrassment and laughed when I couldn't stop myself from being sick again.

Okay, maybe not. One of my co-workers graciously took care of it for me. I went home and rested up and felt fine in a day or two. I really appreciated that somebody who wasn't my mom would do that for me. Nobody even brought it up when I returned to work.

Even so, there's not exactly a graceful way to come back from that. Because of the gracious way they all handled it, I don't carry it to this day as a social scar. It's a funny story, but damn, I would have liked to have looked a little more like a grown-up and less like a dumbass kid who can't even manage to get to the bathroom before being sick.

———————

There isn't really a cute way to wrap these stories up with a pretty bow and push them out, showing you how I'm actually an incredible man and deserving of your respect. That's really actually the point. There is nothing worthy of a pedestal to be found in this chapter.

Nobody is perfect, and a lot of terrible things happen to people all the time, whether due to their decisions, the decisions of others, or just bad luck. And that's okay. It gets ugly when we try to hide these things and pretend that they didn't happen because we don't want to tarnish our reputations.

By all accounts, these episodes could and should have been cause for great pain and embarrassment and shame. It was the ways that people around me responded that freed me from those possibilities. Bryan could have come back and told his brothers and everyone else that I needed diapers after I sharted myself. My coworkers could have made a running joke out of me throwing up in the hallway, asking security for a copy of the tape. Even Terrance, despite being kind of a dick, could have made a more intentional effort to further sabotage my opportunity at love. Instead, he called me after that trip didn't go as planned with the girl and told me it was okay and that we would have to do more things like that with just the guys.

Sometimes circumstances allow us the power to free people from their shame before it ever materializes.

Is It All Dead?

Christianity is a bizarre, complex religion that invokes a lot of different thoughts from different people based on their own experiences, backgrounds, places of origin, etc. Allow me to take a moment to define Christianity, at least based on the way I was raised.

There's this big ass book with all of these rules that must be followed at all times. The book is too large to actually read, but a couple times a week a pastor (who is most certainly a man) will tell you everything you need to know. You'll find him in an old, run down building (or maybe a fancy, modern one these days). He will likely "teach" you by focusing on all the rules you broke more so than teaching the content itself.

The gist of the book is that somehow a white Middle Eastern guy named Jesus lived a long time ago and died and probably came back to life and that makes it okay that you did a shitty thing last week and the week before and so on. But you're only safe if you ask him to forgive you of these shitty things. And only if you ask for forgiveness *after* doing them, because they can't be premeditated. And only if you're sincere. And it all needs to happen before you die.

If you were to die before having a chance to say sorry, then you're screwed. If you confessed before sinning and then messed up, the confession was disingenuous and you are screwed. You better be confessing immediately following any acts of sin, or you are screwed. It's also an unforgivable sin to have tattoos, drink alcohol, vote Democrat, or be against the death penalty (the same thing that ironically got Jesus killed). And don't even get me started on those homosexuals.

If we're being honest, this doesn't sound very interesting and certainly has a limited appeal. It definitely doesn't sound like the foundation to a meaningful existence framed by the freedom of Jesus's teachings. It sounds more like a cult summer camp, complete with weird campfire songs and some odd-looking Kool-Aid that is passed around the circle with each of us drinking from the same cup.

For some people, Christianity can be hurtful. For me, it became boring.

———

When I was a kid, I loved going to church. I would ask my parents if we would "get to go" all the time. Are we going Sunday morning? Sunday night worship service? Wednesday night for Kids group? The all church game night this Friday? I was passionate about being there as much as possible.

But was I really passionate about church itself? I remember thinking the music was a bit boring. And it was hard to stay awake for so long with someone just talking at you. I remember walking swiftly (never running!) out of the sanctuary as soon as service was over and hanging out in the church's gym. Or rushing out to my parents' car after service, cranking the dial to 10 on some almost-cool Christian music while my friends hung out with me.

Things became more serious when I was in middle school. I remember going to a church camp for the first time. It was really exciting to be in a large group of people worshipping the same God with music more attuned to younger ears. The fact that there was a drum set and a speaker system meant that this place was absolutely rocking compared to my normal church experience. Not to mention, camp food—this was before the theme park incident so I only saw the junk food as good in the eyes of the Lord. But the thing I remember clearest?

The Holy Spirit "shakes." There's some *Christianese* for you. This is something that isn't very unique, based on conversations with other people. Here's how it happened for me. The camp had several sessions or services where the band played, and there was a sermon, and I think every single one of them had a "coming to Jesus moment" where you were brought to a literal crossroad. You either confessed to Jesus your need for forgiveness or denied the need and essentially implied, "I'm good," and continued to live your heathen life until you died. At which point, you were rolling the dice on your eternal destination.

It's pretty easy to make the right decision when said in no uncertain terms such as these, eh? Naturally, when one of the services had a response time, I went down to the front altar area to pray. I'm not sure what the sermon was on. Probably about how we all need Jesus 'cause Hell is hot and swearing is sinful. It was middle school camp, which basically meant it was very little about who Jesus is and much more about fire insurance.

Whatever the case, I was praying whatever was on my mind and I remember that I felt this sensation in my stomach and chest. I started to tremble a little, as if I had a slight shiver. It was like time stopped, though it certainly didn't last more than five seconds. How to describe the feeling... have you ever been in a shower with two shower heads? You can put one shower head on hot and the other on slightly cold. It's a pretty awesome sensation to turn them so you experience both washing over you at the same time.

It was like my soul was feeling this awesome warmth while a bucket of cold water was poured over me. I did my best to hide it, but I also cried. I conspicuously wiped my elbows across my eyes, stood up, and walked back to my seat. I don't think I told anyone what I experienced.

Was that the moment the Holy Spirit came into me? Yeah, maybe. Was I dehydrated under the hot summer sun and hungry because lunch was hours ago? Probably. Was I just caught up in the moment and confused by the spectacle around my twelve-year-old self? That's almost certainly true. It could be one and not the others, or it could be all three. Either way, I got the shakes, so my faith was confirmed as real. That's what somebody later said about these types of experiences. It couldn't possibly be that I was afraid of a Hell that sounded much worse than the Hell I was already living while being bullied at school. I thought I finally got my "Get out of jail free" card.

That moment could have been one of the most defining moments of my life. Instead, it felt weird and maybe even scary. And it wasn't even the most memorable part of camp that year. My favorite parts were actually capture the flag, winning an annual 5k race in record time, and hanging out with pretty girls. And a buffet at every meal. Those are the moments that I remember clearest. The shakes were more like an obscure movie you recall from your childhood only to find out that your buddy saw the same movie. You thought you were the only one who had a personal, authentic connection to that movie, but it was actually just a product of emotional manipulation and some intentional production.

Youth group was the same shit in a different setting. I loved the youth group I was going to in Colorado Springs. But in truth, most of my favorite moments had more to do with fun and goofing around rather than life change. I had some real close friends, but it all lost my interest when they graduated high school and left (they were a couple years older than me). If anything, I may have turned out a bit jaded by the whole thing.

I'll own it. Some of it was me just being a teenager and not really knowing who I was. I struggled with who I wanted to be (cool, hot, smart) compared to who I actually was (awkward, lonely, uncertain). And some of it was the bullshit of the pressure placed on us to have the right answers and to not do the wrong things. If you can memorize the passage from Song of Solomon the 7th chapter, then you're in. Obviously, not that actual passage. Song of Solomon was treated like Biblical porn. It's in there, so we unfortunately can't delete it, but we're going to ignore it as much as possible.

That altar call business I described at camp was still being done at every major youth event and Sunday morning service. And I think I went up and prayed at pretty much every single opportunity. If I had a dollar every time I got saved I would have been able to make this a movie instead of a book. Then I realized something. It was the same people down on their knees next to me at damn near every altar call. It was one of two things:

1. We were all just doing what we were expected to do.

Lift your hands when singing without thinking about the words you're saying. Go down to the front and kneel and confess every wrong thing you've done since the last time. Turn around and hug the people around you, praying for your soul in whispers and hallelujahs. Walk out and repeat next week.

2. We were all scared for our eternal life.

Dear God, I am going to sin this week. I don't have the courage to not smoke or stop looking at porn or not kiss my girlfriend or all of the above. Don't let me die before I can repent of my sins.

Okay, there's nothing wrong with this. Oh wait—yes, there definitely is!

I think that most everybody around me at that time had great intentions. Several of them are truly Godly people. It becomes a problem when the goal is to create these grandiose, emotional moments and no life change happens. It's manufactured and fake. Or when the only way you can convince someone that your religion is right is by telling them they are doomed to death if they choose any other option.

That is not Christianity. If it were, I bet Jesus would have had way more violent, hardcore moments where he would have called fire down to scorch the earth around the Pharisees or taken the sword from Peter's hand and sliced through Judas himself. Instead, he did the opposite. His badass moments included taking the sword away and healing the injured attacker. His rebellion was to bring peace in the face of crucifixion rather than return the favor of violence.

But I was never taught that about Jesus. Church was the same song and dance over and over again. And it was all dead. It was empty. I couldn't feel anything in this. I became immune to the fake highs and the fake lows that were supposed to trick me into feeling God. It worked for a while, but once my mind realized what was happening, it all went numb.

Just like summer camp, my fondest memories of youth group included activities with no spiritual focus at all. In its place, the itinerary included basketball, rock concerts, and more pretty girls. I didn't talk to many other teens a whole lot about Jesus, but I remember passionately telling them about the new music I was listening to.

And I felt so much shame and guilt around this. I saw through the thinly veiled propaganda and that made me feel like an outsider. I believed that God was real and Hell was real. But I didn't buy into the system that was built around them. I thought that there had to be a way to experience God, but I couldn't find it in all of this. Maybe it wasn't the system that was broken. Maybe it was me that was broken?

———

This really makes a very good point that we shouldn't ignore. Despite my ignorance and brokenness, I still kinda turned out okay. It gets a little shifty over the next couple years, but I landed on my feet just fine. People want to act like you can't find your own way; if you start wandering, you're likely to choose the path to the gates of hell. Everyone calm the fuck down!

Turning out okay had nothing to do with my Bible memorization or the prayers I muttered at the altars all those times. It had nothing to do with hymns that I couldn't delete from my memory no matter how hard I tried. Or terrible metaphors that demonstrated a woeful ignorance of physics: there was a skit done one Sunday in which a Christian stands on a stool and another person who is symbolic of a non-believer stands on the ground next to the stool. They grip each other's hands and the Christian does everything she can to lift the heathen from the mire, but sadly it is much easier for the person on the ground to pull the Christian down. The idea was that we should really ponder if God would consider it wise to be friends with non-believers.

Here's another idea. Maybe the Christian shouldn't be standing above anyone, but instead should be down in the muck with everyone else. Like when Jesus gets accused of hanging out with drunkards and partiers. He was building relationships that pissed off the religious of his day and seems to continue to have that effect to the present.

As if Jesus knew what he was about, the thing that brought me through it all was relationship. I know where you want me to go with this, but I can't faithfully do so. I'm not talking about a relationship with Jesus. That's just not true to what happened with me at this stage in my life. I didn't feel like Jesus was literally "there with me" in my darkest of times. I wanted to feel that way, but it never really happened. In hindsight, I can see how God was working in my life, but it wasn't always so obvious along the way.

The relationships that got me through the tough times were friendships. Some of them were with Christians. Some of them were with non-believers (*gasp!*). Good people create good friendships, even if they don't agree with you on everything. I didn't need my friends to believe all the same things as me, I just needed someone to be there when I felt like I was all alone.

I didn't need a sermon or an altar call or worship music. No judgment if that has worked for you, but I needed someone to be present. If we want to make a difference in people's lives, we should stop preaching at them and start living with them. It's not a Christian's place to point out anybody's sin if they don't know that person, have an understanding of their story, and have the trust of that person to thoughtfully critique their lives.

If my best friend seriously told me I was sinning with how I managed my money or with the vocabulary I used, we would need to talk that out. If a complete stranger did it, they don't know shit about me.

The pressure to evangelize in that way to strangers creates cycles that only manufactures shame for both parties. The accuser feels shame if they don't call out other people's sinful lives because what kind of Christian wouldn't do everything they can to save someone from Hell? And if the Christian does speak up and the person doesn't repent, then they must have done it wrong. The accused feels shame over the supposed sins they've done that they can't overcome or they feel embarrassment over being harassed by someone who doesn't understand them.

Instead, let's use the Jesus model and share some food and drink with the people we care about. Let's become friends. Not projects, just relationships. Let's talk about whatever comes up organically. If that's Jesus and the ways to live a better life, great. If it's music or sports or the best Mexican restaurant in town, then also great. But let's not bring undue shame on each other, especially because of bad theology.

———

At this point, I would imagine that several readers think me a heretic doomed to hell. That's a damn shame that you would consider someone a heretic just because they believe something different from you or used a couple words that made you uncomfortable. In fact, this is yet another way in which I have found myself feeling shame. For some time, I felt a deep shame over my beliefs, because I felt morally wrong by the standards of the church culture I was a part of even as I knew I was pursuing Christ.

That's really absurd, considering the heritage of our religion. If you know much of Christianity, you have likely read the New Testament. After Jesus died and ascended to heaven, he left behind a rag tag group to carry on the legacy. And it all went to hell quickly. Peter (and others) wanted to make it so anybody that joined this new movement had to adhere to Jewish laws. Some of these laws became unnecessary, such as the dietary laws. Eventually, it was revealed to Peter that maybe even circumcision was not necessary. But there were many who refused to accept this change.

Circumcision was a requirement to be a Jew. Problem was that Jesus brought a message for everyone. Who in their right mind would want to give up their current beliefs, get their dick sliced, and then get ostracized from their family? Doesn't sound too appealing, and it wasn't needed to follow Jesus. His message was that "God so loved THE WORLD."

So, Paul comes on the scene and basically wrecks it by petitioning for this to be let go by the early church. Circumcision is something that was done for generations. It was absolutely necessary to be included as a follower of God. It was similar to traditions we have today, like baptism or Communion. If somebody were to suggest these things should be released so that nobody need do them anymore, they would be crucified faster than Rob Bell (you may recall that he became a popular punching bag among Christian evangelicals when he wrote a book called *Love*

Wins that posits the absurd notion that Jesus wants everyone to get to heaven regardless of their beliefs. The audacity!).

So, Paul and Peter and everybody else have a big powwow called The Council of Jerusalem, and it is determined that circumcision is not needed to become a Christian. Paul was being a real heretic there, and could have felt deep shame—I bet the establishment tried to taint his reputation by suggesting that he was well intended but sadly deceived. Instead, his theology was determined to be closer to God's plan than what the establishment already held. And now nobody needs to have their penis cut to be a Christian.

There was a status quo, a requirement that was previously universally accepted. Paul and Peter and James (the brother of Jesus who acted as a trump card at the meeting) wanted to let as many people into Christianity as possible. This is what my life was missing. I wasn't taught that God could reveal himself to me in ways out of the tradition. I didn't know that I could explore things outside of what was "written in stone" to learn the truth of Jesus.

As I got older, I realized I really shouldn't be bored with Christianity. I became bored as a coping mechanism to cover my shame for being different and to cover my guilt for not understanding God the same way as the people around me. it followed me everywhere I went and I heard the same sermons ad nauseam. I believed in the Bible, but was unsure about the things I had been taught. It didn't feel real anyway, so I might as well push back some and learn.

The best thing that could have happened to me did. I started to ask questions and research answers through books. If reading is not your thing then check out audio books, Ted Talks, podcasts, and interviews: whatever answers your questions. Just don't back down from asking them. For me, I read books that were controversial in Christian circles. I found myself suddenly excited again and interested in the things I thought I knew.

I found that Rob Bell's aforementioned *Love Wins* actually wasn't heretical in any way. How is it heretical to ask questions about the reality of hell and why it might break from traditions? I hate the idea of people going to hell; help me understand the purpose of it in God's plan. The questions Bell asked were also the questions I was asking, and I have a feeling neither of us hold much fear of Hell and we are both still trying to figure things out.

More importantly, maybe I'm *not* trying to figure it out. Maybe I don't think about hell at all anymore, because it seems like God is more concerned with how we as Christians should bring heaven to earth. Maybe the ones destined for hell are the ones who bring hell to others' lives by peddling sex slaves or through buying products made with slave labor. Have you recently purchased a smart phone, a t-shirt, a movie, or cheap food? Then it's likely you've benefited from slave labor, as have I. Thank God there is grace for all of us.

Soon after, I also read *The Bible Tells Me So* by Peter Enns. For so long, I had issues with the Bible and the ways it contradicts itself. Even the birth of Jesus is told in four different ways that directly contradict each other at times. There are ways to explain this, explanations that have been provided by preachers and professors for generations. There are also interpretations that approach it from the perspective of being written by multiple authors for multiple audiences. That creates a different version of the same story. If my audience for this book you are reading now was my mother, I would have sworn a lot less. If I had written it to be a New York Times bestseller, maybe I would have cut out all the heavy religious stuff. I wrote it for myself and for you, so my approach changes, and the details remain truth but serve a different purpose.

I continued this habit and found books on homosexuality in relation to Christianity. And then I read some material on racism. I found content on sexism and arguments for women being preachers (something the churches I grew up in would never have approved of). I stumbled upon resources that debated if pacifism should be a requirement of a Christian. I read time and again that materialism and greed were the sins holding many of us back from the life that Jesus came to provide. My eyes were being opened as I continued to search for truth.

———

I once read an article about a history teacher who wouldn't assign students homework directly related to specific historical events. Rather, the assignments would be focused on research methods. Instead of doing a paper on the invention of the printing press, she would have the students pick their favorite invention that was at least 50 years old (a student might pick the guitar, for example) and they would do a paper on how the item they chose came into existence. As they learned the methodology, then they could better understand how to learn about the printing press when that information was needed. Learn the methodology of how to ask questions about God.

God is truth and truth is God. If we believe that God is the Creator and the all-encompassing Being then there is no truth out there that can exist apart from God. So, feel no shame over your inquiries. Feel no guilt or embarrassment over the things that don't make sense to you. Ask the question, no matter what it may be. And if you're not sure there is a God, still seek truth. Truth is universal.

Was it evolution and not creationism? Is it okay to be affirming of gay people? Does music have to be a certain way to be "Christian?" Do I need to be baptized, and if so, which method is the proper one? Did Jonah really get swallowed by a whale or was that just a metaphor? Remember, if nobody had ever asked questions then Christians may still require pantsing to check who is a part of the kingdom. But the questions were asked and were pushed and were not dropped.

This is the way I found freedom from shame over doctrine and theology. The good news came when I recognized that ALL truth belongs to God. We don't have to be afraid of studying things that run contradictory to what we think is true right now. If challenging facts arise that disprove what we believe to be true, then it is not the truth that has changed but instead our understanding of what is true. I expect that there are things still in me that I am missing or ignorant of. Hopefully they will be revealed to me this year, or next or someday much later in life. That's the point: it's a journey towards truth. And wherever truth leads, I hope to follow.

It's challenging to determine what truth is, because it is not synonymous with facts. Facts are sterile and can be proven empirically; truth can exist in fiction and hyperbole and is sometimes difficult to prove. You can feel truth. What I do know is that all truth belongs to God and truth is not boring or shame-bringing. Truth transcends life.

It would take many more years for me to further comprehend this, and lots of heartache that would arise from my own misunderstanding of God. When you lose faith in your heritage, you may lose faith in God and find yourself feeling ashamed. For me, the shame I felt would lead to many more regretful moments in my story. But the truth of Christianity is that God is always for you. Even with this realization, it would take a longer journey for me to finally let the shackles of shame fall off.

V

Where There's Smoke...

When I was a kid, my parents split up. I don't want to get into the gritty details, because I feel like that is more their story than my own. Few details were shared with us kids anyway. I was the eldest at eight years old, so it was more something that was just happening to us rather than a sequence of events that we could understand. It did not feel as if we had any real influence over the circumstances. All I will say is that there was a breach of trust that led to a schism between them and a time of separation where my siblings and I bounced back and forth like a pinball machine. Sometimes we were staying with Mom and sometimes with Dad.

Considering my young age and a general uncertainty around why this could be happening, a lot of the details remain very blurry to my memory. I think it was springtime for most, if not all, of the separation. I remember watching cable TV at my uncle's (where my dad was staying) and seeing some old movie with a scene where vicious apes attack humans in a cave. I believe it was one of the original *Planet of the Apes* movies. It's hard to say, because I can remember so little of that time frame. I would guess that it was only a matter of a few months, but it's not something we talk a lot about as a family. There's a sense of "don't ask, don't tell" that envelopes the topic. I don't think it is cowardice or fear that makes it as such, but rather a desire to let bygones be bygones.

Which is absolutely fair. My parents reconciled and have been married for three decades and counting so far. That is one hell of an accomplishment. And I really don't feel any shame over that. If anything, there's a sense of pride and gratefulness in them overcoming the circumstances that caused so much conflict in their relationship. Reconciliation is always a beautiful story. The shame is instead how I had felt and responded in the years following.

Despite remembering very few details about this time in my life, I do remember finding the upheaval of my family structure to be very upsetting. I didn't know it was going to be temporary. In the midst of it, I had so many thoughts about how this could be my new reality. That's a difficult feeling to manage for adults, let alone an eight-year-old child. I wanted so bad to know what the problem was so I could fix it. How could my parents be separated? Who was to blame for this?

I am confident that there is plenty of blame to go around, but as a child I almost completely blamed my dad. I had a few reasons, but they were all shortsighted and unfair. He was the one who moved out of the house, though I doubt he wanted it that way. He also seemed to be the angrier of the two and I very much had an "allergy" to raised voices and aggression. High emotion conflicts such as a marital separation are likely to cause a lot of raw emotions, but I sympathized much more with my mom's tears than my dad's pain-induced anger.

It's just not possible for a child to parse out all the complications of a struggling marriage, never mind the fact that I knew very little of the whole story. My judgment ultimately fell down on my dad's shoulders. I blamed him for all of it. I didn't ever confront him as a child, but I held onto that resentment for years.

It wasn't expressed in an overly brash way. I tend to be conflict avoidant as much as possible. But I made very little effort to connect with my dad in ways that we could have both enjoyed. There have been many missed opportunities. Ironically, this behavior actually led to a new source of shame, albeit to a lesser degree than many of the other topics within this book. See, my dad is very mechanically gifted and capable of doing any type of handyman work that you can imagine. From the simplest of things such as a quick oil change to installing cabinets in my kitchen to completely remodeling my parents' entire home, his skills seem to know no bounds.

I do not have that gift. I have very few ways in which I fall anywhere near the stereotypical "Man's Man." I could have had a relationship with my dad in which he taught me all of these things. I think he really wanted to, but I always acted indifferent and unengaged and even inconvenienced when he would ask for help. I don't put any value in a silly definition that suggests that you *need* to be a car guy or handyman in order to be a man. That's all bullshit. But I do wish that I personally knew how to do these things. Had I made the effort, I would have learned such useful skills and felt more comfortable doing things with my dad. This chasm between us would lead to stunted growth through my adolescent years, and not just in the realm of odd-job expertise. Without any guidance or adult perspective, I would especially struggle with female relationships, sexual attraction, and puberty in all its awkwardness.

————

One thing that I absolutely carried from my childhood years was a desire to rescue a girl. That's probably a pretty typical desire for most young men. I saw my mom hurting and I thought about the ways I could help. So, any time I noticed a young woman in pain, I would gravitate toward her and try to find a way to save her. Quite frankly, despite women being equally strong to men, I think that desire to help can be a very good thing. And when done with pure intent, many times women do appreciate it.

But there's a healthy way to do it and an unhealthy way. I went with option number two: I genuinely wanted to help but there was no real sense of making a difference. If I saw a girl crying, I felt too awkward to go up with a box of tissues and just ask her if she was okay. I was so afraid of rejection that many times I wouldn't do anything at all and would instead just watch her from afar. I would daydream about the ways that I might help her and how she would obviously want to reward my help with a kiss or some other display of affection as a sign of appreciation. My insecurity caused a genuine desire to help to instead have a hint of a predatory Savior complex. Being that I was too shy to act, it never got darker than that. But I would find myself obsessing over that girl for weeks on end, until I came across another girl in a similar situation who "needed help."

This perspective was shaped in my middle school years and evolved on the same path through high school. I didn't date a lot as a teenager. I had crushes and infatuations and even had a girlfriend once or twice, but never for more than a few weeks. I believed I had fallen in love about twenty times, often repeating the same girls in cycles. These feelings were rarely influenced by chemistry and commonality and were much more frequently triggered by attraction and that continued desire to be a rescuer.

I would "fall in love" with Amanda, and when she didn't seem super interested, Brittany would catch my eye. When nothing happened there, I would remember Amanda and the things I liked about her again. Add in Chelsea and Danielle and whoever else and a cycle was formed. Between a fear of rejection and abandonment and a purity culture that implied that even my dating habits should be monogamous (though it was actually referring to marital status), I found myself on a high-strung roller coaster of emotions.

I didn't have the courage to actually express these feelings to these girls. This led to a lot of wall-flowering, just hanging out in the background and trying to subliminally get my feelings across via telepathy and then being frustrated when feelings were not reciprocated. Which, in turn, led to a very unhealthy addiction that I would use as a means to fulfill my desire for intimacy.

Most people are probably expecting me to say porn. For clarification, I have never actually watched porn. Even that phrasing feels questionable, like I am trying to protect my reputation in some way. I don't say that from a place of righteousness. Feel free to keep reading and see, I only seek to clarify. My true addiction was masturbation and I didn't feel the need for porn to fulfill my cravings.

For some reason, people tend to distinguish between porn and masturbation. I actually don't think there's anything terribly wrong with masturbation—it's pretty natural and can be done in healthy ways. But I was addicted. There was no hint of health in what I was doing, especially from a mental and emotional perspective. I would do it compulsively any time I felt depressed or lonely. I would need that kick of dopamine and would masturbate without even thinking about whether I *should* do it. So, while there are some potential distinctions between porn and masturbation, I readily believe there was no real difference for the sake of my story.

I didn't disrespect women I didn't know who were being used behind a camera. Instead, I essentially did the same thing with the lens of my imagination, many times dehumanizing and disrespecting women I did know. Does it matter that it was only in my head? I don't think so and for that I am sorry.

Jesus said that lust was the same as adultery, which was punishable by death at that time. His point wasn't that he would want to kill me, but I think he was making the point that just because I am not physically harming someone doesn't mean that there isn't harm being done to my own psyche and the way I am viewing women as something to use rather than someone with their own agency and human value. I feel his grace much more than any sense of condemnation, but this season of my life definitely put me on a path of unnecessary pain.

A side note of humor for a moment. A year or two after high school, I was talking with a pretty girl on MySpace. I have to admit that I don't remember her name at all. The whole thing was very innocent and short-lived. We had actually met each other a couple years prior at a pool party that a mutual friend was throwing for a birthday. I had gotten to know this girl after she had visited our youth group a couple times in the months following the party and never saw her again. When I was 19 years old, I bumped into her unexpectedly while she was working at a Christian bookstore. I was perusing the new music of the tiny metal section when she walked by. I remember thinking she looked decidedly more punk with her black-dyed hair. This was a couple short weeks before "the incident," as it shall forever be known.

How many juicy stores start out at a Christian bookstore? You are being completely naive if you don't think that happens way more than you or I know. For me, it all happened like a quick montage in a Rom-Com movie where you know you have met someone that is going to change your world forever. I reintroduced myself in case she didn't remember me. We both awkwardly shook hands with reddening cheeks and accidentally interrupted each other trying to fill the quiet by asking how the other had been. And then the store's audio system played "In Christ Alone" as we both silently smiled at each other for a moment that seemed like it would never end. The spell didn't break until she was paged over the intercom by a co-worker.

Later that week, we reconnected on social media and were catching up a bit through private messages. It was all timid and chill and going seemingly well. After the typical questions about how work was and all that, we started to dig a little bit more into some personal details while still maintaining a degree of timidness. They were surface level questions like, "what's your favorite food?" Or, "who is your favorite band right now?" Like I said, it was all very innocent.

It wasn't Instant Messenger, so this whole conversation ran its course over several days. It was a situation where I would wait for hours on end for a response, hoping that the fact that I loved tacos didn't somehow turn her off to the continued conversation. Although if tacos were a problem, then it would have been doomed to fail from the beginning.

At one point, she asked me what my deepest, darkest secret was. In my defense, that's quite a provocative fucking question right there. I can't speak for her, but twenty-year-old me was awfully curious by what the "right answer" to that question was supposed to be. Should I tell her that I occasionally eat a slice of cheesecake with a slice of pie on it and ice cream atop that? Or something titillating like how I had a secret crush, but was too nervous to tell the person? Or show my darker side by confessing that I once considered murdering a classmate.

Okay, so I made that last one up. But you must see my point about just how absurdly wide the spectrum of possible answers could run. I probably should have just told her I was a closeted poet. Girls love poetry and it would have given me an opportunity to showcase my writing skills. Based on personal experience, I now know with one hundred percent certainty that telling her that I was struggling with lust was not the winning response. I didn't even say it in a way that set any dirty expectations, or at least I don't believe I did. If so, it definitely wasn't intentional. But the crux of my message was that I was addicted to masturbation.

I was just desperate to talk to someone about it. I was getting my ass kicked in an uphill battle and knew I couldn't do it alone. Should I have told a girl that I thought I wanted to date after talking with her for just a few weeks? It doesn't take a rocket scientist to do the math on that one. My response was likely either going to create an awkwardness that would cause her to never talk to me again or some sort of sexy proposition that would have been much more than I could have maturely handled at that time.

So where does the story go from there? You could probably guess. We talked it out, went on a few dates, had a great relationship together and amicably broke up years later. Things didn't work out, but we still stay in touch to this very day and catch up over coffee once a month.

Yeah, that didn't happen. I never heard from her again.

The shame I feel around this circumstance was not scarring, but it's very indicative of just how naive and uncomfortable I was. It didn't take me long to see the error of my ways with Christian Bookstore Girl, but I did feel deeply embarrassed by who I was. The lesson that I learned wasn't that I over-shared too early in this potential relationship, but rather that things I struggled with defined who I was. And the person I was could not be desirable to the type of woman I wanted to be with. I felt deep pain and I felt completely lost in how to navigate the dating scene from here. I may as well have been a blindfolded kid swinging at a piñata that hasn't been lowered to within reach.

Obviously, that's not where it all started—I was already in the middle of the mess by then. Nobody's sexual journey really starts when they are twenty years old. It's much younger. I'm no expert, so I don't rightfully know when a sexual journey truly starts for anyone. But I'll start as early as I can recall with the events that influenced my own experiences.

I don't have kids and I don't have any education in childcare, so I'd be remiss to offer any parenting advice. I do know that this is one of those areas where my parents dropped the ball a bit. I'm not exaggerating when I say I never once got the sex talk from anyone, including my parents. I think they would have found it to be very uncomfortable. And that message was reinforced by the church culture we were in. Nobody talked about it at all because it was a dirty thing and we don't talk about dirty things.

Whatever the case, I literally have never had the birds and the bees explained to me. Maybe that wouldn't have changed much of my life story. After all, I've had the good fortune of never having a sexual act physically forced upon me. They were all my doing, more or less. So maybe getting the talk would have led to the exact same decisions. Who knows?

I do know that 12-year-old me was entirely enamored by the beautiful young women in my class, and it came out in some unhealthy ways. I loved sports and numbers and rating athletes based on their skill sets and individual attributes. It seemed natural to adopt the same method in observing the girls around me, so a buddy and I would do that frequently. *She is absolutely a 9 out of 10 and would be my top choice.*

I would rarely speak to these girls and never had the courage to ask a girl "out" or to be my girlfriend. The risk of feeling rejected didn't seem like it was worth it So instead, I would continue to observe. I didn't understand relationship at all and thought everyone obsessed over their crushes the same way I did. I couldn't compute how people started actually dating. It was beyond comprehension.

So, I would continue to be smitten time and again, all while piecing together my own sexual education with the limited understanding and resources I had. There were computers at school that we could use for certain classes, including my first-ever study hall in 7th grade. We only had dial-up at home, so the internet seemed really freedom-inducing. You could even watch video on it; the technology was amazing.

As I said, I was also obsessed with sports. I would visit the Dallas Cowboys website frequently to read the latest articles on the team and how the season was going. At some point, I found that a section of their website was dedicated to the cheerleading squad. This was a startling discovery. The girls around me were pretty, but this was next level stuff. These were pictures of gorgeous, grown women posing in bikinis under waterfalls.

I would literally spend my hour-long study hall browsing through hundreds of pictures on the team's gallery. After seeing all of those pictures, I came to the realization that other football teams had equally interesting websites. This isn't a one-time thing; I would guess I did it a dozen times or so. My teacher and classmates were *literally* five feet away from me.

I was smart. I would only do this on the computer that was turned so I was facing the classroom and had a wall at my back. My teacher was none the wiser. One of my buddies got caught because he used a different computer in the same room and it wasn't well hidden. I don't recall the punishment, but I definitely thought he was stupid for getting caught. And I kept on doing it every chance I got. I felt some guilt, but not enough to stop.

I also did something I am quite ashamed of now. This habit and the underlying struggles started to manifest in the real world. I remember one time I was in the hallway at school and was walking behind a girl that I definitely thought was smoking hot. The hall was quite crowded, and I intentionally brushed by her in a way where I inconspicuously but intentionally grabbed her butt.

I don't know if she knew it was me, but she definitely reacted and made it clear she didn't appreciate it. Even if she didn't react at all, that's assault, brotha! Seriously, it was a disgusting thing. I now have a lot of thoughts on that and will readily admit that it was unacceptable behavior. I don't know what inspired me to do it, other than thinking she was hot. I don't believe it was really even premeditated.

But I did feel great embarrassment and anxiety about getting in trouble. I knew it was wrong. It is never okay for anyone to do something like this. It is unacceptable and not "cool" or "manly" or anything along those lines. It's also not just "boys being boys." Learn some fucking respect. It became clear that I had to and that I was not quite the pure good guy I thought I was.

Oddly enough, despite my blatant unhealthy fascination with women, I still had not delved into masturbation at all. I didn't really explore what to do with these confusing feelings and emotions for years. I'm not sure why I risked staring at a computer in a classroom without taking further action. But in a weird way, I felt ashamed of my innocence and unawareness on this, too. Everything I did felt like a loss.

There was a conversation that took place in middle school in the cafeteria. I always sat with the same five or six guys. I made them my "group", even though I was definitely bullied by a couple of them. I had accepted the hierarchy and I rolled with the punches, sometimes literally.

One time, they were all talking about Britney Spears. She was very popular then and was just becoming a bit of a sex icon as she distanced herself more and more from her Disney beginnings. I didn't know a single thing about her except that her music was on the radio and I wasn't a fan. One of the guys made this boisterous claim that he heard that an absurd amount of cum was found in her system during some undefined medical exam. Obviously, this is some dumbass, over-the-top middle school braggadocio talk and nothing more. But everyone at the table spoke up about how impressive (?) this feat was. I said something about how crazy it was to have that much in one person. I got called out.

The guy said to me that I didn't even know what "cum" was. And the truth of the matter is that I didn't! I told them that I thought he had said something about *gum*. You know, like how Britney's style of music was called bubblegum pop. I associated the two and assumed that's what we were talking about. I am not making a joke at all, that is literally what I thought at the time.

They all laughed at me and my lack of knowledge about sex. It was middle school; they were all knuckleheads that didn't know anything more than a couple dirty words for semen. But I felt like I was more clueless than anyone else. Somehow the joke went from her being skanky to Josh being a puritanical virgin. Logic couldn't help me see the absurdity of their jokes. I felt like I was on the outside.

Later on in high school, there was another conversation in another cafeteria. This time it was at my private Christian school. Some guys and girls were talking about how many times guys could masturbate in a single day. I would guess the guys wanted to impress the girls by proving their stamina and the girls wanted to impress the guys by their willingness to be present for this type of conversation. With a little bit of juvenile sexual tension on the side to add some intrigue.

Up to this point, I still had never intentionally masturbated. I had healthier relationships with the people around me compared to the middle school experience. Nobody at the table was bullying me during recess. I was a peer instead of a victim and was accepted for who I was. But I still knew there was no way in hell I was going to tell the truth that I had never masturbated. I didn't have a fear of bullying, but beet red embarrassment was only one stupid spoken sentence away.

So, I made something up about how many times my personal record was. I said four times in one day, just going for something in the middle of what everyone else was saying. Whatever would allow me to not have to participate further, but also not get picked on. It was the right thing to say as the next guy nodded approvingly as he proudly announced he had done it seven times in a day before. And nobody thought twice about my answer.

I somehow managed to feel shame about sex and masturbation from nearly every angle possible. I felt guilt over the fact that I looked at girls and thought about them in ways that I was told were dehumanizing. I was ashamed that I was not enough of a man to pursue the girls I had real feelings for and instead allowed myself to just look for the next possible crush. I was embarrassed that I didn't know *more* about sex and didn't have the same type of experiences that they all had apparently lived. I felt like an outsider in every way. And this would all lead me to a deeply hurtful relationship that I would refer to as one of the lowest points of my life.

VI

...There's Fire.

There was a knock at the door. I was in the bedroom of a woman I had been seeing for the better part of a month. She had an apartment all to herself, so I couldn't help but wonder who was at the door. We hadn't ordered any food or been expecting anyone. She told me to wait there for a moment while she checked it out. I probably should have gone with her just to make sure everything was okay, but the thought didn't cross my mind. I stayed seated on the bed, scanning her room. I remember looking at a shelf of movies and thinking about how much fun it would be to watch all of these movies for the first time as a couple. Things weren't official yet, but it seemed like I had finally found the love of my life and I fixated on juvenile romantic gestures like that.

She had walked into the hallway and headed to the front door, closing her bedroom door in the process. I didn't really hear anything and wondered who was out there. I never did get the story on what exactly happened, but it was a few minutes before the bedroom door was opened again. To my dismay, her ex-boyfriend was the one in the doorway. And we were both shocked. I was not expecting him to find out about us this way and I saw absolute confusion rush over his face in a wave. We knew each other, though not well. Even so, I suspect that I was the last person he expected to see in his ex-girlfriend's bed. The fact that I was fully clothed and he had no business being there didn't matter to him. He came at me.

I've already expressed that I'm not a fighter. And he was being aggressive, but seemed to be attempting to toe the line between aggression and fighting. No fists were thrown, but we scuffled and pushed and shoved our way outside the apartment complex and to our cars. There was a lot of confusion and raised voices along the way.

For some reason, this dude thought she was still his girl-friend. I was under the impression that they were absolutely and without question done with each other. He was also under the impression that I was sleeping with her. In truth, I was in love with her, but we hadn't gotten anywhere near that territory. I was still a virgin at this point and was stumbling my way through the make out game, none too confident about anything beyond that.

It all happened so fast that I couldn't make sense of it. But I do remember feeling the weight of shame when I recounted the story to my roommates. I walked into the townhome we lived in with only one shoe and no winter jacket despite it being winter in Colorado. My roommates listened intently as I stumbled through a barely coherent retelling of the night's events. They asked if I was okay and if they needed to come with me back to the apartment where it all happened. They were insinuating that they were ready to throw down for me, but I knew the girl was okay and I didn't want to risk further escalation. Embarrassment ran amok in my mind as I saw flashbacks to that scrawny middle school kid barely surviving the locker room. I got punked and felt heat on my face as I headed to my own bedroom to call it an early night.

I think it is likely that everybody has at least one relationship in their past that they reflect on and it causes them to sit back and lace their fingers behind their head and then throw out their hands in an open, uncertain gesture and just mutter, "I know, it doesn't make sense." Even if I told the whole story in every minute detail, it still wouldn't be logical. I won't make any excuses; I want to be transparent about every mistake.

This was a mistake, probably from beginning to end. She was a sweet girl who I'm going to call Sara. We had worked at the same company for a year, though on different teams. She was leaving her job at the cafeteria on the campus where we worked, so we exchanged contact info. She had been dating this other guy who also worked there. Sara had caught up with me a couple times in the previous months leading up to this time, but out of respect for her boyfriend, I hadn't put another thought into it and assumed that the exchanged contact info was for the sake of being friends on Facebook. I had interacted with her boyfriend in casual conversation a few times over the past year and liked him alright, as well.

Sara and I started talking via private message (damn social media at it again!), and she disclosed that she was newly single. I asked if they were absolutely done and she confirmed that they were officially broken up with no intentions of reconciliation. I felt like that meant I had the green light. So, we started getting to know each other; I didn't make any obvious gaffes like with the MySpace girl, and we met up for coffee.

We were both relatively broke, so many of our dates were just hanging out at her apartment and watching a movie. I'm sure it won't come as any surprise that I had a tendency to fall in love quickly, especially with someone who was reciprocating my attention and interest. It was a matter of weeks before I started saying that "love" word to Sara. In hindsight, I was about 22 years old and still had a naive understanding of love—I think I knew that, but my feelings were authentic.

Things were going great until that night with the knock at the door. After that, we continued to text each other but I didn't see her for a couple weeks. She said she needed space to clearly and unambiguously wrap things up with the other dude, so I would oblige her that. But I also told her I would never stop fighting for her love. So melodramatic, I know. That's how relationships are in the early stages, right? If it's not an external conflict like this, then it is an internal conflict complete with self-doubt and fear. Of course, I was double dosing in this case. I texted her repeatedly and invited her to a Christmas party my family was hosting.

She was noncommittal and only decided last minute that she could make it, along with her mom and brother who were visiting from out of town. It seemed to go perfectly; my family liked Sara and her family seemed to like me. It was destiny. I had been waiting my whole life and this was what I had been waiting for. But I still didn't see her again for a couple more weeks as she spent time with her family until they went back home. Finally, she told me it was over with the other guy and that it wouldn't be a problem any longer. We were together at last, boyfriend and girlfriend. Nothing was going to stand in our way now.

We spent so much time together. I would see her 4-5 nights a week during this time. This only expedited my ever-expanding love for her, and I, no joke, started talking about marriage a month later. That's when she dropped the next bombshell on me: she was technically still married and waiting for her divorce to go through with her estranged husband—not the guy I've already mentioned.

That should have been a red flag to pump the brakes and take a step back. I obviously at least slowed things down, right? Wrong! I now saw this as a chance to save the damsel in distress from not one, but TWO douchebags. This was practically my wet dream. I would finally be a hero that no one could question. I would just wait out the paperwork for however long that took and then we would get married.

I really didn't consciously think about it all this way, with me being a knight in shining armor. I wasn't that arrogant or had any sense of a white knight type of complex. I was just going with the flow and thought our relationship was an amazing thing for both Sara and I. Counseling sessions, great books, and talking with wiser people than I through the years would later reveal so much that I was blind to.

Sara was hesitant to plan out too much long term, but we did have extensive conversations in terms of what we hoped for out of life. She talked about how much she loved Colorado and how thankful she was to no longer live in Missouri. I told her that I hoped to someday be a successful writer. We watched movies together and in a particularly excessive moment of immaturity, I gave her my high school class ring. That's a sweet thing to do when you're eighteen. She was older than me, in her late twenties, and must have found this silly despite the sweetness behind it.

None of it seemed to matter when she dumped me the day after Valentine's Day. Yes, that is how fast this all happened. I am not condensing it to only hit the main points. It was all a matter of a few months. Apparently, she had decided to get back with her ex-boyfriend who wanted to beat my ass at the beginning of the chapter.

This was the week before my birthday and I fell into the obligatory funk sitcoms tell me I am supposed to. I felt like a shadow of myself. I called out sick from work a few times and stayed in bed until noon. When I was at work, I would occasionally see him and he would make sure I saw the smirk on his face.

I felt isolated. I deleted her number from my phone. I fell into that type of depression where time doesn't exist. You get up when you're supposed to, eat when you're supposed to, go to bed when you're supposed to; you do these things out of habit, not because you feel a thing. I spent every moment I could with friends. I didn't want to talk about it at all, but I also didn't want to be alone. We would play video games and watch movies. I tried every trick I could think of to distract myself from my feelings.

A couple months later, I was awakened by a text message notification on my phone. I groggily sat up and looked at the screen, wondering why someone would text me so early. It was Sara's number. She had a different area code than all my other contacts, so I knew right away. She said she missed me so much and wanted to see me again.

Let's get one more really good "Josh's biology is always trying to destroy him" story. A couple days after the text, Sara came by my townhouse. We quickly retreated to my bedroom, avoiding my roommates. We talked a little bit, but I don't remember it being all that meaningful. It seemed more like a conversation to fill the time and reacquaint ourselves to each others' presence. And then we started to make out. It had been two months since we had seen each other and it felt like forever.

There were a lot of pent up emotions, likely for her as well. It wasn't wise to jump straight into kissing and moving without talking first about what was happening. She still had her boyfriend and was still married (as far as I was aware). I still had no commitment from her that these things were going to change.

I have no idea how long we were making out, but she started to touch me in ways I had never been touched before. In our previous time together, we had some rigid rules about where and how we wanted to touch each other to avoid going further than we wanted to. Obviously, she was previously married, but I had still been a virgin and my childhood had taught me that this was one of the most valuable things I had. The rules had worked great in allowing us to have a good time without unwanted pressure, though in hindsight I'm not sure she loved that arrangement.

But on this day, we didn't communicate anything about this before we started making out. And because this was my first serious relationship up to this point, we were now going above and beyond anything I had ever experienced. And it was intoxicating. I didn't have a single thought in my mind. I was a leaf on the wind and it would take me where it saw fit and I was prepared to enjoy every moment.

Something unexpected happened. I was leaning over Sara when I suddenly saw a drop of blood fall on her face. I leaned back slightly and touched my own face. For no apparent reason, my nose had started to bleed. That was quite jarring and broke the spell I was under. I got up and cleaned my nose off to stop the bleeding. There's no mood killer like balled up toilet paper stuck up your nose to staunch the blood. Sara and I laughed about it all and talked for a couple minutes and she left. I guess it was all just a moment of weakness and nothing more.

That's the story of how God saved my virginity with a bloody nose. Maybe I'm being facetious. It's perhaps more likely that the extremely dry spring air in Colorado was the cause. That happens to me from time to time. Whatever the case, I did not catch the hint.

Sara and I texted back and forth for a couple days. I developed a theory that she kept going back to her boyfriend despite their unhealthy relationship because they had had sex with each other and I couldn't contend with the type of bond that creates. Sex creates a unique bond that can't be accurately imitated or substituted. I need to own this. As far as memory serves me, this was entirely my idea and she did not prompt it at all beyond the aforementioned make out session that ended so unceremoniously.

But she agreed with me, enthusiastically in fact. She said that I was probably onto something there. The obvious solution would be for us to have sex together. If we were ever going to have a real chance to make this work, we would need to do the deed. A night or two later, I got a hotel room and we had sex. That's how I lost my virginity to a woman I thought I loved who had a boyfriend and a husband.

There's really more to that story, probably on all sides of it. I even gave her a couple hundred dollars a few days later because she was struggling with her rent. I'm not sure how I'm supposed to feel about that exchange of money, but it certainly sounds seedy. All of this is my perspective on what happened and it is likely limited due to lack of information for the parts where I was not present. I do know that I made a string of terrible decisions that I regret. Sometimes people say that they are glad for the mistakes they have lived through, because it led them to where they are now. If someone were to ask me if I would go through those things again to get where I am today I would say, "Fuck no!"

There is no way in hell I am going to say that I was happy to have had sex with a not-yet-divorced woman while she may or may not have had a boyfriend she was cheating on. As a Christian, there are a whole lot of sins I gave into in that moment. Adultery is a heavy and tragic sin, according to the Bible. Jesus took it a step further by saying that if you have even lusted as a married person or after a married person, then you have committed adultery. No need for the distinction for me, because I had sex with a married person.

For a minute, I really thought that meant right then and there that I was doomed to hell unless I got my shit together ASAP. I wondered if I had lost all my value after losing my virginity. I was told for years that this would be my gift to my future spouse and it was by this gift that my marriage would be perfect and God-ordained. Purity culture put so much weight into this that for months on end I continued to try to make it work with Sara despite my deep pain and her waning interest in me.

And to be clear, I was a Christian during this whole thing. I wasn't a good Christian by most people's definitions, but I absolutely believed in Jesus. I believed every single thing I was "supposed" to believe to be a Christian. None of that had left, though my desire to lean on my beliefs had withered away.

I had come to believe that I had enough of life figured out to know what was best for me. I needed Jesus to save me from hell and I would save myself from the hardships of life. I wholly admit that I was making choices based on my own wisdom, and I didn't really feel Jesus's presence through that time frame. I do not believe that he had abandoned me, but I had made my decisions and needed to see my own folly before I could really appreciate his direction.

I also know I wanted to feel Jesus at that time, but all I felt was his absence. I'm not blaming God for this, but it is true. What do you do when you don't feel God? I found myself wondering if there even was a God! Anybody who pretends there is an easy answer to that feeling is likely trying to sell you something, whether it is a product or a watered-down Gospel. It's something that should take wrestling and struggling and searching. And it's okay to not know the answer.

All that to say that I am thankful that I came through on the other side. I am not sure how real the threat was, but I had considered suicide as a means to escape the nightmare. Not only did I not kill myself, but I also found myself more whole afterward. I didn't feel a need to be in a relationship again. It was a long process, but I started to feel comfortable in my own skin instead of tailoring myself to look like someone that I thought could attract a girl.

A funny thing happened when my future wife, Dannika, and I first started talking a few months later. We knew each other from high school, but in sharing my story I was able to understand hers more as well. We had both gone to some dark places and that made us closer to each other once we started to date. I didn't need to be in a relationship, I was healthy alone. And it made me enter into a relationship in the right way and find the love of my life. I don't believe for a moment that God wants us to go through evil things. I do know that he used it to reshape my future.

This chapter wouldn't be complete without a check in on the effects this all has had on life today. I'll ask myself the stereotypical church question: *Where are you on your spiritual journey, brother?*

I haven't figured everything out and I still don't live a perfectly pure life. Some people struggle with porn their whole life and I can't claim to be much different. Paul states that despite asking God multiple times, he was never relieved of a thorn in his flesh. He doesn't specify what sin of his had become such a long-lasting thorn, but it doesn't really matter; the point is that Paul was the self-proclaimed chief of sinners and still managed to write two-thirds of the New Testament.

There is no justification for my struggles, other than to say that I know what I want out of life and I also find myself praying to God to relieve me of my sins that I continue to do. I wouldn't even say masturbation is my worst sin. I also would say that I don't think it is universally a sin, and I know that there have been times in which I committed no sin while completing such an act.

However, I remember having a conversation with my wife not long before writing this chapter in which I told her that I was isolating myself from her by masturbating when she wasn't around. What we shared in intimacy, I was manipulating and making my own. It was very difficult for me to tell her, because I knew what I was doing was self-centered. I was choosing to forego our intimacy for my immediate, empty cravings. It was difficult to tell her, because I was deeply ashamed. I thought that when I got married I would no longer feel this temptation. That was naive of me and I was wrong.

But most importantly, it was hard to tell her because I knew it would hurt her. For many months, I told myself I would overcome it alone and she would never need to know. This would be the least hurtful way to move forward. Instead, the shame continued to grow within me as my resolve to tell her diminished.

This is not the trademark of a healthy relationship, whether with God or people. But talking about it is. So eventually I mustered enough courage and told Dannika. And it was an awful feeling. It was embarrassing and disappointing and hurtful. And yet, she also made it clear that despite it certainly being a problem, she also forgave me. The issue wasn't what I was doing: masturbation is not a big deal. The problem was that I was being selfish and my actions were taking away from the sex life and bond that we shared.

It seems that we as individuals have the power to remove shame from others. People, like myself, already place enough shame on ourselves. We don't need an extra helping from someone else. Dannika could have emphasized my shame, but instead she showed me the grace I needed to feel true freedom. In an unexpected turn of events, I received a message from Sara not long after this moment of confession that I shared with my gracious wife. Sara apologized to me for all the ways she had wronged me and put into words her own shame over the mistakes we both had made. And I was blessed with an opportunity to model the grace my wife had provided to me by in turn providing grace for the person who had hurt me. There was no Holy Spirit "shakes," but I did indeed start to feel God once again.

VII

A Complex with Complexity

"Smear the queer" was an oddly named game I used to play as a kid. It was a chaotic, violent blend of football and tag and was honestly some of the most fun I ever had growing up. You grab as many kids as you can along with a football and whoever is holding the ball is the target for everyone else to tackle. That person remains the target until they are tackled to the ground and fumble the ball. The next person that picks up the ball becomes the new target. No real objective other than to avoid getting crushed and to hold the ball as long as possible without getting tackled.

In high school, the local movie theater raised their ticket prices by a buck or two. Everything already felt so very expensive for my minimum wage job that paid $5.15 per hour. Whenever anything like this happened, I would always say derogatorily that it was gay.

As said in other chapters, I wasn't allowed to swear. It was basically punishable by death. Teenagers are teenagers, so we would find other ways to jokingly prod each other or yell our frustrations at the X-Box. I don't know how many times I have called John Madden a "freaking faggot" because of his video games.

I never directed this at a homosexual. At least, not to my knowledge. Then again, if somebody was gay, I doubt they would be comfortable enough to share that with me only to have me call them a fairy or something ignorant like that. I'd like to think I wouldn't have reacted that way, but maybe their concerns would have been valid.

At any rate, they were *just* words; we didn't mean anything by them. Bear with me for a minute. Notice the context in which I used these words. Clearly, I was using these slurs as synonymous with something being stupid or dumb.

That doesn't mean it's okay. This is a book all about shame, so I want to be clear that I'm including this in here because I know better now. But it is interesting that I wasn't allowed to say swear words, yet I don't ever remember getting in trouble for saying these words. Maybe I never got caught, but I think more likely it just wasn't important to the authorities in my life. Perhaps there is a second aspect to this. I was raised to believe that homosexuality is a sin. This was not up for discussion, and truthfully, I never really questioned it much. If homosexuality is a sin and gay pride is a thing, then "those people" are not just sinners but are in fact proud of their sins! It was deemed that simple and this perspective was further solidified as it became a political issue that Republicans oppose.

Gay people were categorized as gay people by the culture around me to define that they were a mass of people in their own right. It's similar to how we considered all Nazarene church attendees to be a part of the in group without knowing anything else about them. It's normal to use defining distinctions like this to understand sub-groups of various cultures more extensively. That part is just fine. It becomes a problem when you think that is all there is to someone, like they are *only* gay or only a Christian or only a Hispanic person, et al. It gets even uglier when you use those definitions to determine who is out.

This type of over-labeling is flawed and doesn't allow us to see things for what they are. For example, my favorite restaurant is a little family-owned business in Colorado Springs called El Taco Rey. So, their name gives away some things about what they offer, but I haven't given you any details about it. If you don't like Mexican food, you probably aren't going to be a fan (you're also just wrong). But what if you like Taco Bell? Does that make you more likely to enjoy a place that makes their own tortillas and has the most amazing enchiladas smothered by award-winning green chile? It is fair to call both Taco Bell and El Taco Rey establishments that sell Mexican food. That's the end of their similarities. If restaurants deserve a higher degree of nuanced dialogue, then certainly politics, religion, and people are that much more deserving.

Upstate New York is a highly conservative part of the country. It is very rural and very predictable in its demographics. Farmers. Blue collar workers. Middle-aged. White. Conservative. There is not a single thing wrong with all of that, except for the way in which I can remove the complexity of people in just a few words.

I have heard so many people say things like, "You can't be a Christian if you are a Democrat" or "Pro Life people don't care about babies, only fetuses." Hell, sometimes *I* have said those things. That's really messed up. Obviously being a member of a political party has nothing to do with your religious beliefs. Your faith should inform your political ideology, but they are not the same thing. There is not a religious party and a secular party.

Painting caricatures of mass people groups makes for good headlines and may even prove a point you think is accurate, but it's never going to gain the trust of hearts and minds that is necessary to make a real difference. It will only get cheers from your crowd and jeers from the opponent.

It would be really easy to write a chapter on all my political beliefs and my personal history that led me to these beliefs. I would guess about half (maybe more) of you would find those beliefs to be well-thought out, reasonable, and generally correct. And the other half would hate my guts and think that everything I had written before this chapter was interesting but is now invalid because I'm a ****(place favorite "othering" insult here. If specific words come to mind then you have some work to do).

How obnoxious are politics? It has the ability to wreck holidays, friendships, even families. The right answer isn't to ignore it or pretend it doesn't exist. But it does bring up a thought I have on identity. I would contend that one of the biggest and most disruptive sins of our society today is found in the ways that we look to simplify people with singular labels.

———

We find comfort in simplicity. There is nothing wrong with that. In many ways, maintaining simplicity is a very healthy thing. There are numerous resources on finding happiness by simplifying your schedule, your house, your life, etc. There is a whole movement happening in which people are selling their suburban homes and purchasing tiny homes in secluded areas. Sometimes it is a financial decision, other times people are paying more for less and still finding greater happiness.

Simplicity is also a healthy thing for human development. When I was a child learning math, I just needed very basic formulas (and very basic grammar, apparently). Don't lead with all the exceptions, just the general rule. Once I understand that, then I can learn the correct ways to break the rules.

$1 + 1 = 2$

That is a fact. It is always completely true. It is not up for debate, even if you are that one asshole that is in every group that wants to debate everything. There actually is a debate about that formula but it's not taught to the average math user, because for all intents and purposes the simplest understanding of the formula is the most functional. Take that teaching method and apply it to other areas of learning like language, science, and history. There are numerous examples where "it is what it is" works, and there aren't any counterexamples that deserve attention. It is helpful to communicate foundational information this way.

The problem starts to creep up when the realization dawns upon you that contradictions are not a bad thing, and complexity adds to the tapestry instead of being an agent of chaos. The foundational pieces may be concrete and well defined, but the further you build upward the less simple it becomes. And that problem is amplified when faith and philosophy are taught with the black and white scale that harbors simplicity.

It is not good to be a Republican or a Democrat or a Libertarian or a member of the Green Party if you think it means you have to match the party line on everything. You don't have to agree on everything with any one of these. It is okay if your opinions genuinely line up word for word with the Democratic Party, but don't be lazy and think you need to agree with every one of their platforms because you are concerned with climate change. Don't think you need to be a Republican because you are a Christian. We are all more complex than that. It is a lesson I am still learning.

———————————

I never understood this need for nuance even into my early twenties. Maybe I had a growing awareness, but it was still minimal and I will readily admit that I was still ignorant. It was around this time that my understanding of gay people was challenged. I thought I knew what I believed, but I didn't actually know any (openly) gay people and didn't know a thing about the community as a whole.

Then, a crazy thing happened. I started meeting gay people. I met an awesome young man named Sean when I was going to college at Eastern Nazarene College. He was black, gay, and an absolutely incredible person. Suffice to say, he was breaking paradigms that my almost exclusively white, conservative upbringing had built. We became good friends and spent a lot of time hanging out with the same group of friends.

I've known several gay people since then and don't feel it appropriate to compile a list. But I found that they are more than just gay. They are also writers and actors and athletes and cooks. Some of these awesome people care a lot about poetry and social justice and Harry Potter and are Christians or atheists or didn't give a shit about any of it. That was confusing. It turned out that there were just as many variations of gay people and what they believed as there are of any other people group.

So, I read a lot. I came to a few realizations. I had come to a place where I was able to acknowledge homosexual people as more than that one part of who they are—like finally recognizing a football player is not *only* a football player, but that they also have favorite songs or hobbies or brands of underwear or political ideologies. I have since come to realize that they are *so much more than* that—"they" meaning whoever you think about in simple terms. They are more in the same way I am so much more than white or Christian or bearded.

That's not meant to minimize the importance placed on being gay by homosexual people, either. Obviously, sexuality is a uniquely important identifier for anybody. But it is not the only identifier.

C hristians like to argue that a gay person cannot be a Christian, because it is a lifestyle of sin. I need to call bullshit on that. I don't believe that being gay is a sin and I would recommend *The Gay Debate¹* by Matthew Vines as an article that acts as a great starting point for any additional research. That being said, I know many will disagree with me and I want to add a perspective on sin in regard to myself.

At this point, it is clear that I have lived a lifestyle of sin my whole life. I have been prideful, sexually active in destructive ways, gluttonous, hateful, greedy; the list goes on and on. At no point in my life could I say that I even for a season lived a sinless

---

1   http://www.matthewvines.com/transcript/

life. I am still a sinner as I write this. There are days where I will readily admit I question God's goodness and I have way more faith in my own thoughts than anything godly. I judge people as much as ever, it's just different people that I judge.

That's the whole point of the Gospel. According to Romans 3:23, "All have sinned and fall short of the glory of God." There are numerous scriptures that use similar language. By the standard set in The Holy Bible, I am able to guarantee that you still have sin in your life. If you can't think of one, then lying would be a good place to start your list. All this to say, if sinners can't be Christians, then we are all fucked.

The good news is that Jesus came for the entire world, sinners of all shapes and forms. Obviously, this is not a deep dive on biblical scholarship and interpretation. I'm not looking to change your mind on your beliefs. I want to change your mind on *how you view* your beliefs. I have been guilty of keeping my faith as simple and black and white as possible to maintain functionality. It worked for a time, but it is not designed to be the entire journey. I would challenge you to read and study more from perspectives that you disagree with. It's okay to continue to disagree afterwards, but you'll know that you actually believe what you believe instead of assuming that the hand-me-down faith your pastor spoon fed you wasn't just their opinions.

———

As I said, in my estimation the greatest sin is labeling people with one dimensional definitions. For my part, I believe that sin should be defined as an act that separates you from God and community. The Bible attempts to reveal what that looks like through specifics, but it is hardly exhaustive, and is not always universal. It is not intended to be a rulebook, but rather a foundational starting point to understanding God.

Labeling others from a simplistic viewpoint may or may not hinder your relationship with God. God is, after all, an invisible being in the sky and any sense of closeness is nebulous at best. However, labeling others will undoubtedly interfere with whom you are capable of experiencing community with. How can you maintain a sense of community with all of God's creation if you are going to exclude some based on only a portion of who they really are?

If there are whole people groups that you refuse to interact with, then you are creating an exclusionary community in ways that Jesus never modeled. If your only interactions with certain people groups are hostile and violent (violence isn't always physical), then you are disrupting community.

I have found it hard to talk earnestly about politics and religion with people who hold a strictly conservative view. I disagree with so much, and instead of digging into the nuance, it feels safer to divert the conversation to trivial topics like sports and food. I am also finding it hard to speak with people who are considered extreme liberal leaning, as it seems that any added nuance to the opposing view is regarded as defecting and requires a "circling of the wagons" perspective.

I don't like debating with people who believe the Bible is inerrant, because they are likely to label my views as heretical and may even suggest I am not a Christian and will be doomed to hell. See what I am doing? These are real thoughts I frequently have about others. I am minimizing people to one aspect of who they are and am stopping the fluid and healthy movement of the community. All because I am assuming the worst. I told you I was a sinner, even by my own definitions.

When I first started my journey, I saw the world in its simplest form: black and white. As the world was revealed to me as more complex, I felt shame over my simple views. I felt shame that I casually used words like queer, gay, and faggot. I didn't need to be told these words were offensive, because I could see in the eyes of my gay friends that they were hurtful. Then my own eyes were opened to how I was excluding them above and beyond my thoughtless language. I was confused that I held faith in a God that had enough grace for everyone, but couldn't allow gay people into the community. I was guilty of thinking that I could somehow hold more grace for people than God, because I cared for these people. The more time I spent with my gay friends, the more I realized that they were good people and I couldn't help but think they were holy and were children of God just like me. It led me to read and study more, digging into Godly sources to discover that God wasn't the problem but rather my own simple view of God was the issue!

Though I am embarrassed by the things I did, I have found that the shame I held had a beautiful solution. Interestingly enough, it was something modeled by Jesus himself in that holy book. He didn't see people as one dimensional. He talked to tax payers and prostitutes and violent revolutionaries and saw what they were beyond these labels. He sat down and ate meals with them and saw them in their fullness as the creation of God. And in seeing them in their fullness, he was able to talk about things that mattered.

As I began to view people holistically, something changed about my own perspectives towards myself. I thought that I was damaged goods, because I had lost my virginity in an affair with a married woman. Virginity is irretrievable and no amount of repentance could change that. But fully seeing others opened my eyes to how God saw me. I was still a child of God and still capable of being in a meaningful relationship that did not have to be ruined in any way by my past mistakes. I saw my own full humanity and saw that I could still be fully integrated into the kingdom of God.

Through my own reconciliation, I have become inspired to pursue more reconciliation than I could ever have envisioned. I don't want to engage in hostile dialogue with the "other." I want to see them for their full humanity the same way Jesus did. I have no doubt that Jesus would fraternize with Republicans and Democrats and bigots and communists and he would see God in them despite whatever horrible things they may believe. I want to meet those same people where they are and I want to do it over enchiladas and tacos and burritos. Some people are gay, some are drug addicts, some are political activists, some are Christians, some might be all of the above. But *everyone* loves good food and good company. We shouldn't be surprised: it's just like Jesus to show us the path to salvation for the community of humanity.

VIII

Re-inventing Heaven

When a Christian dies, they grow wings and fly up into the clouds and play some badass harp tunes. Everybody knows this. Heaven is this perfect place removed from this world where dreams come true and nothing wrong or terrible ever happens. No one will ever go hungry or thirsty. Imagine a place where you will never need food or drink ever again? What a wonderful world. There will never be a desire or want that is not already fulfilled.

Worried about what you will look like? Don't bother with it. Your body will be perfect. But not by our definition here! No, it will be perfect by the eternal definitions God will have structured in place. Which means we will all look like babies in diapers like Cupid on those cheesy Valentine's Day cards. Or maybe we will be orbs of light with earthly-like heads so we recognize each other.

At any rate, there's no point in being shamed by your looks, because everyone will be naked anyway. It's going to be like a godly South Beach at Spring Break: no shoes, no clothes, no problem. It will be the biggest, funnest, nakedest party ever!

Except there won't be any sex, because you won't have any more bodily needs and there won't be a need for reproduction. Plus, nobody wants to get it on to nothing but harp music 24/7. I'm sure the only singing will be hymns, none of that modern, post-contemporary hipster bullshit.

Man, why does heaven sound so much like hell?

I used to feel a lot of shame around heaven. Most people feel more shame about hell, or feel like hell is their likeliest eternal destination because of the shame that they feel. That's not how it works. I don't believe that God really ever uses shame to bust someone. It's not like he's up in heaven saying, "Ha, she cuts herself, she doesn't treat her body like a temple. Yup, she's screwed. Off to hell with you!" That's absurd. What an awful God that would be. It's scary how many people believe in a God that closely resembles that caricature. No wonder Christianity is so painful for some people.

And yet, this is how a lot of us grew up. Memorize the Ten Commandments. Memorize any verses that cover the to-dos and don't-you-dares. Memorize and recite verses verbatim so you'll never forget them. Do any of the sins you just memorized and it's off to hell with ya.

It's no surprise we have a hard time believing God is a loving God. If I had a girlfriend who treated me that way, my friends and family would be up in arms about how unhealthy the relationship is. God doesn't use shame to get us to behave. Shame is something you feel when something didn't go right, when you feel morally corrupted based on your community's standards. It could be from something you do, but it could just as easily be from something that was done to you. I feel shame sometimes over my timidity. Or over my inability to actually feel good about my finances. Or over the time I lost my virginity to a married woman.

God doesn't use shame to fix you. You feel shame because you need help. Maybe you need help and guidance from people to get through it. Maybe you need an internal help, because you need to learn to do it on your own. More likely, you're like me and need help from a greater being and a greater good that I have come to know in Jesus.

So, what did it say about me when I didn't want to go to heaven? Seriously, read the beginning of this chapter again. It sounds truly horrible. On a scale of "let's do it now" to "no fucking way," I was definitely much closer to the latter. I felt shame through that. And a sizable dose of confusion, too. I believed in the grace and love of God and knew that He wanted what was best for me. But it didn't sound like the final destination was going to be all that great.

You're talking to someone who loves metal music. Everybody knows that's the devil's music. It sounds like hell wins in the best rock party category. I want to see a mosh pit where people are jumping all over the place and running in a circle pit and screaming from their lungs at the breakdown. I have sung enough renditions of "How Great Thou Art" and "It is Well" to last me a lifetime. Eternity? Say this in your most Brooklyn-Italian accent possible: forget about it.

There won't be food or water? Okay, so some of these aren't necessarily biblical in case you haven't noticed. But it's what I was taught. If you want to convince me to check something out, just say that there are some really phenomenal tacos nearby and I will definitely give it a shot. Seriously, it doesn't matter what else is going on if there are tacos. Why the hell would I want to go somewhere where I will never taste food again?

And no sex? What do you even say to something like that? I once went twenty-two years without sex. Sure, it was my first 22 years, but I say it still counts. I don't plan on ever doing that again. No judgment on anybody else's lifestyle, you're welcome to be celibate if you like. But I'm quite comfortable with my decision to have more sex, thank you very much.

A lot of people think heaven will be like the Garden of Eden, because that was what life was supposed to be like. The concept goes that this is what it was like before Adam and Eve ate the apple and opened up the Garden to sin, so that's what it will be like when everything is restored. I'm not sure I necessarily agree with that logic, but yeah, maybe that's how it works.

So, will there be food and water in heaven? Probably; they had that stuff in the Garden. Will there be sex in heaven? Maybe—Adam and Eve seemed to have a lot of kids in like the very next chapter. They could have been doing it in the Garden. Will there be rock music? Hell yeah!

———

I once read a phenomenal book by Richard Rohr called *Things Hidden*. In truth, I suspect any book written by him is likely brilliant. In this one, he shared this concept about how the very best things can't be explained—they are driven by experiences.

That very concept is mind-blowing when you relate it to things you have felt. People ask what it's like to fall in love or to hold your newborn baby. The answers usually involve a lot of stammering and ambiguous language around our feelings, but there is no succinct, universal answer that fully encapsulates the beauty of the moment.

That's how my feelings started to evolve in regard to heaven. At some point, I just realized heaven isn't anything like I was taught growing up. Instead, I started viewing it as "my" heaven, where everything is what I love. Rock music and burritos and going one-on-one with Jesus on the basketball court. You can have your heaven, too. God will somehow pull some sci-fi interdimensional shit so that you can have your heaven and I can have mine and we will miraculously still be together.

I finally figured it out and wanted to go to heaven. Awesome, no more shame. It sounds like this great place with all of my favorite things and maybe even all of my favorite people, too. I don't know who gets to heaven and who doesn't. Truthfully, I'm not too worried about it. I want everyone to get to heaven and I'm certain I don't have more grace than God.

I once read a funny joke about this in Shane Claiborne's *Irresistible Revolution*. The story starts with Peter checking people in at Heaven's gates. At some point, he turns around and looks inside the gates and sees way more people in there than he is letting in. He sends two angels to investigate. They come back to him later and inform him that Jesus is on the side of the wall on the outside whispering to "heaven's rejects" about a little side door that gets you in. Jesus is the only way to heaven after all. If he makes exceptions, who am I to argue, right?

I had finally found an understanding of heaven that sounded appealing. Before I didn't want to go to heaven, because it sounded awful. Now that heaven sounded great, it seems like I should want to get there ASAP. Instead, I found I still wasn't in any hurry. Something funny happens when you're in your early twenties: you get this overwhelming sense of invincibility and brazenness. I just wanted to live forever. Life seemed like this wondrous, unexplored thing. Adventure and positive energy are around every corner. My early twenties were pretty subdued by most standards, I suspect. But they seemed absolutely perfect for me.

I lived in a small townhouse with three other guys. There were a handful of other friends who would come in and out like recurring characters in a sitcom. We would stay up late watching good movies and playing video games. We ate out more than any self-respecting adult would ever recommend. We hiked up in the mountains. We went to rock concerts and jumped around in the mosh pit. It felt like there wasn't a single worry in the world.

It was a little crowded, but nobody seemed to ever have any real complaints about it. It was like living in a dorm, except we circumvented all the typical college rules and managed to only live with people we enjoyed. There was no curfew and only minor degrees of disturbing nudity (we couldn't completely avoid it thanks to my roommate Jon having a fascination with walking nearly naked from his bedroom on the main level to the shower upstairs). When life was this good, I couldn't find it in me to wish I were somewhere else.

All good things must come to an end. There were a ton of reasons for it, but I became jaded about life. I think everyone does to some extent. Personality and circumstances may influence how deep we fall into this deviation, but it is bound to happen to us all.

I had lost my virginity to someone who didn't seem to care about me. I was bored with a job headed nowhere. I realized that maybe I should have gone to college. I had originally skipped it, because it didn't make sense to rack up a lot of debt without knowing what my degree would be in. But since I wasn't really doing anything with my life anyway, it seemed like it wasn't that much of a risk. Some of the jadedness stuck with me. It wasn't just a feeling that is a nuisance later revealed to be fleeting. It became a mindset that clung to me for weeks on end.

One time, my brother and I went to see Flogging Molly in a tiny little dive on Cinco de Mayo (May 5th, for all my uncultured readers). It was a packed house that night. Like probably breaking some fire codes type of packed house. It was 90 degrees and there was about a quarter inch of beer that covered the floor by the end of the show. My shirt was hanging on me like an extra layer of skin to be peeled off. That's the type of clinging this jadedness felt like. It wasn't going anywhere and I couldn't find a way to shed it.

I am married now and happily so. My wife is awesome. I have a job that compensates me well and has been a blessing for my wife and I. My extended family is awesome (both mine and my wife's). I own a house and really have everything I need. But that kid is gone. I don't feel the same excitement in life like I did in that town home. Infertility has been a real bitch to us. Sometimes it's hard to think that I am part of a multi-billion-dollar corporation instead of writing full-time or bringing people closer to the life they're looking for.

I hike up in the mountains that we have here in Colorado. But I never do it enough. It's hard to convince yourself to do it, even when you know it will be awesome. Once I get out there, there's a little breath that gets caught in my lungs and reminds me that we are alive and God is still here. But something changed in me. I once was shamed to hate the heaven I was taught. Then I learned of a heaven that I desired, but I felt guilt over not wanting it *right now*. Then, dissatisfaction settled in and I found myself longing for an escape.

———

I'm not depressed. Or maybe I am, I'm not quite sure. I know there are times where I think to myself that I would much rather be in heaven than here on earth. There are so many stories of tragedy.

Mass shootings.

Genocide.

Refugees dying in an attempt to escape tyranny.

Children starving.

Homeless people in every city.

Women feeling like they have no choice but to get an abortion.

One of my most persistent emotional traits is empathy. Specifically, empathy for the abused or the victims or the mistreated. I am thankful for this most days, but I must confess that there are days when I wish I wasn't so empathic. Sometimes, it's too overwhelming to feel the pain of this world.

This has made me think it would be better to just end it already. I don't want to kill myself. That's a serious matter and nothing to exaggerate about. But I feel overwhelmed by so much evil and destruction. Why do these terrible things happen? Why do *so many* tragic things happen? It is too much and it's not right. And it feels as if there is no end in sight.

It's ironic, because the place that once sounded so boring and unappealing now sometimes feels like the only place to find respite and peace. Maybe heaven is the oasis in the desert where I can finally wet my parched tongue. Have you ever wondered what it would be like to fall asleep and not wake up?

Of course, that's all bullshit. It's the stuff you feel when brain chemicals and emotions overwhelm logic and you can't make sense of anything. And it's completely normal to experience this feeling. But I know the truth. The truth is that heaven may be a grand ol' place, but it's not the place for me yet. It will be someday. I'm holding out hope that our bodies will be indestructible (think Wolverine minus the claws. Jump off a 100-foot cliff, jank the landing, self-heal the broken bones. Rinse and repeat).

The tragedies of this world are very real and are not going anywhere. It's a sad reality. The Bible talks about this pretty clearly. Many Christians believe that things will constantly get worse and worse until the end. That may be true. But the next logical step to that reasoning is then to release all responsibility and ignore the tragedy.

That is ignorant and selfish under any context, but especially in regard to how God would want us to live our lives. I've come to the conclusion that there is a better way to think about heaven. Heaven is not meant to be a place in the sky that is unattainable until we die. True life is experienced when we find ways to bring heaven to earth right now. Feed hungry people. Give water to thirsty people. Give your clothes to the naked. Be generous with money.

I am ashamed to say that I am really terrible at a lot of these things. I am empathetic, but I also tend to be quite the skeptic. Oh, you're homeless? You probably made a string of terrible decisions and the same thing will happen to me if I spend too much time and resources on helping you. If I give you money, you're just going to blow it on booze and drugs. You'll just become reliant on my charity.

Can't you stop having kids? You are clearly not a good parent. You can hardly take care of yourself. Try getting a job maybe. I earned all I have through hard work, what have you done lately? I sound like a real judgmental dick. I'm guilty of having these thoughts more than I care to admit. But there's good news out there, even for me.

I don't have any say in the slightest about who gets to go to heaven, but I do have (at least some, small) influence on if people get to experience a glimpse of heaven on earth.

It doesn't matter if any of my judgments are accurate if I am just using them as a crutch to lean on so I don't have to make sacrifices. When I don't feel a high degree of skepticism, I should give excessively. When I do feel that sense of skepticism up my spine, I should push myself that much further to grab a couple tacos to share and talk to those in need and learn about them and sacrifice *even more*. In truth, that will likely be much more valuable than throwing a couple bucks at the problem.

I am not good at living this way. But I want to be better and strive to do so. I don't think God ever uses shame in any way and He wouldn't want us to use shame against ourselves, either. Shame does not line up with the pure love that emanates from the Creator. At the same effect, I found rescue from the shame I had felt by going through the journey of deconstructing and reconstructing my perspective on heaven. When I was finally able to see my heavenly place was not some unknown time in the future but rather right now, it set me free. To this day, I still have recurring seasons of anxiety about the afterlife. But bringing heaven to earth by serving others continues to be the antidote. When I give whatever I have to someone who has not, whether it be a burger or water or even just a smile, I can't help but feel the shame fall off and be overtaken by the sense that I am where I am meant to be.

IX

The Way to Salvation

Up to this point, almost all of this book has been about things in the past. That makes sense. Most of my life has naturally happened in my first 28 years compared to the last few. Captain Obvious, I know. This is why I have a writing degree and not a math one.

It seems only fair to pick apart my recent history and current events, as well. That's the only way to be remotely fair and honest. In truth, I don't really want to. It's a lot easier to talk about things that have happened versus things that are happening right now. But the more I learn to push away the shame of my past, the more I have become aware of the difficulties of my present.

One deep struggle is that of my normal job. Don't misconstrue it, the company I work for is a phenomenal company. I work at a call center helping people with their cell phones and there is no way in hell I would be willing to do this job for any other company. I cannot fully express the awesome experiences I have had working with this particular organization. I am paid as well as I could have ever hoped for, considering my degree is in Creative Writing (not exactly the most lucrative degree, if you were wondering). The benefits are better than most places: the health insurance plan is real solid, 401(k) matching, an annual stock grant, etc. There is awesome performance-based bonus potential and I've worked with some excellent teams full of good people.

The rewards for strong performance are out of this world. In the years that I have been there, I have been on all-expense-paid reward trips to Los Angeles, Maui, and Las Vegas. These trips are truly VIP-type experiences, complete with gourmet food and exclusive entertainment while staying at swanky hotels. I can't really imagine any other scenario in which I would get to attend a private Snoop Dogg concert. I was able to bring my wife to each of these trips on the company's dime. They showered us with amazing free gifts like yet-to-be released cell phones and ludicrously expensive sunglasses. It is an experience like no other.

I also have become somewhat "famous" within the call center I work at. It's really weird, to be honest. I have had great success and have become a poster child of sorts for incoming employees or people who want to get their performance to the next level. People review my work constantly as a means to find their own methods for improving. Sometimes they sit next to me for live calls and just take notes. Sometimes they did it last week or last month and say hi to me next time they see me in the hall.

It's a center with several hundred people, so it's not uncommon for someone to say, "What's up, Roggie?!" and me to not know their name. I feel kinda like a dick in those times, because

I am not great with names and rarely remember it on my first try. To be fair, everyone is always super gracious about it.

So what the hell am I bitching about? Sounds like I've got it pretty well made. I'm surrounded by decent people while I am very well compensated for my efforts. All of that is completely true. Maybe part of it is more a problem with me than a problem with my job. When I was younger, I thought I knew what I wanted out of life. I was convinced that I would be happy working at any 9-5 job as long as my personal life was everything that I wanted. I had it in my head that I would have a couple kids (more on that later) and an amazing wife and everything else would just work out.

That just isn't very reasonable, at least not for me. Even if all of those plans had panned out perfectly, I would not be fully content. I have come to the conclusion that my expectations for life don't match up with reality. I have dreams of helping people, expressing myself in writing, and being outdoors hiking in the mountains. I don't want to do those things a few hours here and there in my free time; I want that to be my life's work. Reality is not lining up.

I live in Colorado Springs, Colorado. It is one of my favorite places that I have ever been. I am thankful to live here. There is so much beauty with Pikes Peak visible from almost anywhere in the city. There are some great local restaurants. Most of this book was written in about 6 different amazing coffee shops. The weather is just awesome with a nice, warm summer and no humidity. The winters can get a little chilly, but it pales in comparison to my childhood years in upstate New York.

There is one thing, though. I see a lot of homeless and impoverished people. There are quite a few panhandlers downtown and along a lot of the busier intersections. I am sure you have noticed this wherever you live, too. They hold signs saying "anything helps" or "retired vet needs help." By the way, it floors me that the U.S. government will pour $693,058,000,000[1] into our military in 2019 and yet there are so many homeless veterans unable to get the help they need to overcome their physical and mental debilitating injuries.

Whether vets or not, these homeless people are usually really dirty and unkempt and must be so dehydrated being in the hot sun for hours at a time. What a tragedy that we consider people like that to be an inconvenience. It should be really uncomfortable to see homeless people, but it can't end there with that feeling. It doesn't seem like Jesus would respond that way.

The state of Colorado has approximately 10,857 homeless people as of January 2018.[2] That is nearly 2% of the nation's homeless population. Colorado also happens to have an overall population of nearly 2% of the nation's overall population. So it would seem we are about average in regards to how many homeless people live in Colorado. Colorado Springs itself has 1,562 homeless[3] in a city of approximately 472,688.[4] That's a lower

---

1   https://comptroller.defense.gov/Portals/45/Documents/defbudget/fy2020/FY20_Green_Book.pdf

2   https://www.usich.gov/homelessness-statistics/co/

3   https://www.csindy.com/TheWire/archives/2019/05/21/point-in-time-count-shows-homeless-population-leveling-out-in-colorado-springs

4   The overall population is the estimate as of July 2018 found at https://www.census.gov/quickfacts/coloradospringscitycolorado.

percentage, but it is still a sad day when there are so many suffering in our city and our state.

One more statistic for you. Colorado Springs has over 420 churches citywide.[5] And no, that is not a pot joke. That's not even counting other faiths such as Jewish, Muslim, etc. There are also dozens of Christian-based non-profit organizations such as Focus on the Family, Compassion International, Young Life, etc. that are based out of the city. Colorado Springs is essentially the Mecca of conservative Christianity. But that's a shitty thing to be known for. It misses the point. If each church in the city just adopted four homeless people, the homeless epidemic would essentially be solved overnight. But that has not happened and those homeless people continue to suffer. A great prophet once said that we will be known by how we love each other.

Why do we allocate so much time and money to winning a culture war focused on making stores say "Merry Christmas" instead of "Happy Holidays" while a homeless person is freezing to death right outside the doors of our cozy churches? Why do we worry about what laws are on the ballot when there are women who can't afford to be pregnant because their already born kids can't get enough to eat even as we throw away several pounds of uneaten food at our church potlucks? So many times, Jesus did a miracle for a broken body before ever bringing up a single word of repentance. Sounds like a strategy the church should consider next time they are holding anti-abortion signs or picketing against homosexuals or whoever else they decide to bully on any given day.

---

5   http://www.world-guides.com/north-america/usa/colorado/colorado-springs/colorado_springs_churches.html

The good news is that there are people helping. These are people who care and want to make a difference. We have organizations in Colorado Springs, such as Springs Rescue Mission, that are dedicated to ending homelessness by providing a warm place to stay and a recovery program to re-integrate into society. Which brings up the real question for me. Do I personally care? I have the luxury of being frustrated at not having enough time to write, because I am partying on the Vegas strip on an all-expenses-paid trip.

I make very little effort to directly help. I might occasionally donate a couple bucks or a turkey during Thanksgiving. But that doesn't really cost me anything. Sure, it is a few dollars, but it doesn't involve me doing something I am uncomfortable with that would leave a lasting mark.

Instead, I complain about the ways in which I am dissatisfied with not creating enough or doing things that I would deem more meaningful. Interesting that I want something more meaningful and yet make so little effort toward meaningfully helping the less fortunate.

So, what the hell am I doing with my life? I think I am learning, maybe even as I type this right now. I am trying to do everything I want without trusting God. I say I trust Him and I truly do want to be trusting of Him, but my lifestyle shows that I have done as much as possible to remove my need of God from my life. There was a time when I had trusted God very deeply. Probably not on a biblical level the way that Mother Theresa did, but I was taking baby steps in the right direction.

When Dannika and I decided to move back to Colorado from Missouri, we had put a down payment and signed a lease on an apartment before we even got there.

Neither of us had completed a Bachelor's degree at the time. There was not a job between us. We had less than 3 months worth of savings put together to get us by until we found work. We did have the luxury of both sets of our parents living in the city we were moving to, and they absolutely helped through that process, but otherwise we were very much making a leap of faith.

I look back and question what the hell I was thinking. I needed a job fast. I had a couple interviews lined up for the first week I was there, but these were not surefire jobs by any means. One was at a bank that clearly focused on sales (something I had almost no experience in) and another was at a call center doing cell phone tech support (something I had no experience in—it was 2013 and I didn't even own a smartphone yet). To top it off, I was hoping against hope that I would get a job that paid well enough that my wife wouldn't have to find work unless she wanted to. There were a lot of reasons we wanted to do that, but it was largely so she could pursue the things that she cared about at home. We also needed health insurance to come from somewhere.

It seemed like such a long shot that I would not only get a job, but one that would fulfill all of our desires AND happen in the necessary time frame. Unbelievably, I landed the call center position in my first week of job hunting. And it did fulfill all of our needs at that time. My wife has worked at different points since then, but she has been able to choose the jobs she wants and focus on writing and all of her other interests.

It seemed like God gave us everything we had asked for. However, contentment has still been difficult to find. Apparently, I should have asked God for even more.

There's another way Dannika and I have been trying to trust God. Traditionally, the amount of your money you are told to give to the church is 10%, which is a tithe. Tithe and 10% are considered to be synonymous among most Christians, though I think that kinda misses the point.

I would say that the number isn't super important, but 10% a solid starting point if you're wanting to know what to do. The real point is not in percentages, but in how giving and free you are with your money. The bigger sacrifice it is for you, the greater blessing it is. That's true beyond money, as well. The way you give of your time is also indicative of your heart and your love for people. But the Church seems more preoccupied with your money.

As I said, 10% is a good starting point for some people. My wife and I thought so when we first got married. And we had this idea in our head. What if we increased that number by a percent for each year we are married? After one year of marriage, we would increase our giving to 11%. After five years of marriage, we would be at 15% giving. After 15 years, we will be at 25% giving. So on and so forth.

And that's exactly what we have done. We want to increase our faith and reliance on God more each year. And a funny thing has happened through this.

1. We always have enough. We don't necessarily have a lot. There are certainly others better off than us. But we pay our bills

and we have the pleasure of eating out sometimes or occasionally going to a concert or movie.

2. I am still always *fucking* stressed about money!

How is it possible that I could find a way to tangibly show God I want to trust him more, but still find myself more stressed because of those same steps I am doing trying to convey how I trust him! It's a paradox. I wish I could sit here and write that increasing our giving removed all of my anxieties and even enabled us to establish a new soup kitchen and adopt 15 orphan children. That's just not true, though.

Instead, I became more preoccupied with scarcity and my sin was to worry about my financial future. This just may be the most common sin among the middle and upper class in America today. One of the wealthiest people groups at any point in history and we are quite literally worried to death about money.

Anxiety and worry are certainly my own personal thorns in the side. So maybe the problem isn't my job or my massive school debt or the way I spend my money. Maybe the problem is that I think about these things way more than I think about that homeless woman on the corner who would probably be content if I stopped and just talked with her.

What if I just asked her what her name was and how she ended up here? What if I asked him to tell me what he really needs instead of tossing some pocket change at the problem? What if I looked you in the eyes and asked who you really are beyond your shame? What if that is the way to my own salvation?

———

In truth, I honestly don't feel much shame over these perspectives any longer. I have found that the more I have been able to release the shame of the previous chapters, the more I have found freedom in the blindspots that I have yet to discover. The less pressure I place on myself to be perfect, the more I realize God is willing and able to accept me as imperfect.

My lack of faith is a poor perspective on who I am and what I am called to be. But God doesn't hate me or see me as a failure for struggling with trust. Other Christians don't seem to hate me, either. I don't get private messages from people telling me that they are worried for my soul and praying for my salvation. We will see if that changes after I release this book. But even if it does, I will know that those messages would be a reflection of how they view their own mishaps more so than it would impact my value.

Because it seems like the person who judges me the most is me. I feel shame over my self-perception. I am my own harshest critic. Of course, I am hopeful that people read this book and get something out of it, but at this point I am finding that the hardest part is just finishing it and getting it in front of people to read. It seems much easier to give up.

I keep telling myself nobody is going to read it anyway. It is going to ruffle more feathers than it is worth since nobody is going to like it. I will lose respect from people that I have been trying for years to convince I am a writer once they see what my writing is actually like.

For so long, my lifestyle has been one of limiting possible hurt. I rarely ever asked girls out when I was in high school, because I feared rejection. I still play my finances as conservatively as possible and don't ever go for broke—even if it could make all my dreams come true. I don't write enough, work out enough, help others enough, put myself out there and let myself be known enough. I am quiet when I should speak. I say a dumb joke instead of my meaningful thoughts when I do actually say something.

When I was an early twenty something, I had a very handy self-help trick to functionally do the risky things that I knew I should do. I would be on the verge of asking for the girl's number or applying for a job or buying plane tickets to travel. I would feel that pit in my stomach that made me question if this is something I really should do. I would try to analyze every detail and finally clear my mind and just say, "Screw it!"

It only works if you literally say the words out loud. And then I would pop the question, buy the tickets, etc.

I guess that is what this book has become. I am saying my present-day version of "Fuck it!" and putting myself out there. I'm still a mess in my lifestyle and will likely be even more so if nobody bothers to read a book that took me years to write. But I am moving towards my salvation and freedom. I've got plenty more shame to share in the next few chapters, but in my shameful state it is nice to have a brief reprieve and consider the shame that I am escaping with every word I type.

———

I have an ironic author's note I am going to add in the middle of my book here. I didn't write this book in the exact sequence that you are reading it. Some parts were written 3 years prior to publishing it. I have changed as a person even during that stretch in ways that challenge my own words. The clearest example is in regard to this chapter and the practice my wife and I did with our tithing.

We don't do that anymore. At one point, we stopped giving the increased amount and went back to the standard 10%. There were several reasons for it, the biggest being that it became an obligation that I couldn't do with a giving heart any longer. I also felt hamstrung financially in pursuing other things that I felt God was putting on my heart, things that those extra funds could help with.

And several months after that period, Dannika and I decided that the church we were attending was no longer the right place for us to be. There won't be much of that part of the story in this book, because it is still so fresh and "last minute" through the writing process. All that to say, we no longer have a church to give our tithe to and we are very much revamping our whole perspective on what is right and holy in regard to money management.

We feel no shame over it, but I wanted this entire book to be as transparent as possible. We still seek new ways to sacrifice more of ourselves and to give more to others. The theme of this chapter remains unchanged. The way to salvation is not in rituals, even the most beautiful ones. The way to transcendence is in meeting people exactly where they are, especially those most hurt and forgotten. This is a lesson I had learned from spending time with hurt people, but little did I know that my family would soon be the hurting people in need of help as we would go on to experience multiple miscarriages.

X

Broken Dreams

"Our World is Grey" by As Cities Burn

I t was late summer in 2012. Dannika and I had been married for a couple short months. We were sleeping on our queen-size mattress and box spring, minus the bed frame because poor college students, even married ones, can't be choosers. At least we had our own apartment and anything else we really needed.

I was more than content to be married to Dannika. We were in that so-called honeymoon stage, where fights were very rare and a newfound sexual freedom effectively resolved the rest of them. I worked at a coffee shop in a bookstore and absolutely loved my job. Dannika was working at a daycare center. Between the two of us, we barely made enough for our bills while we were in college. It didn't matter. Though we didn't have much, contentment was still easy to come by.

I couldn't say it was perfect, but in a lot of ways it felt as close to perfection as I could hope for. We spent so many evenings reading books and telling each other about what we loved about the stories running through our minds. We learned how to cook for each other and avoid the things that the other can't stand (mushrooms and tomatoes are on my list). And every night, we would have the same routine that ended with us praying together as we fell asleep. It was peaceful, sleeping next to the woman of my dreams. But often times dreams are disrupted.

One morning, Dannika woke up and said something about bleeding. I had never lived with a woman and could only claim ignorance on the subject, but I thought that it must have been something to do with her period. I was very groggy and assumed this must be standard procedure.

Her tone and demeanor, however, was one of uncertainty as she rushed to the bathroom. My levels of concern were rising but I still thought it was probably just "woman stuff." I closed my eyes and hoped that I might fall back asleep until my alarm went off. Time was moving slower than normal as she was in there for several minutes. After ten minutes, I realized sleep was too elusive and I should do my best to make sure she was okay without being too intrusive.

I walked over and lightly knocked on the door. "Are you okay in there?" Her next words would throw my world upside down.

"I think I just had a miscarriage."

Life never goes the way you think it will. It's hard. Damn hard.

When you were in high school, you would plan ahead as much as any high schooler could. You didn't know that you were planning, but there were certain expectations you had for life. We all did that. I know I definitely did. There was practically a check list, even if I never explicitly said it aloud. It's pretty simple:

1. Have a kick ass job.

2. Buy a really nice house.

3. Get a smoking hot spouse and have unlimited sex.

It's the dream of pretty much every high schooler. But I really wasn't *that* shallow. There were other components and dreams that made the unconscious list that were a bit more... respectable. For instance, I also knew I wanted kids.

I actually had a lot of thoughts on that. The number of kids wasn't super important to me. I'd take three or four of them, I guess. I don't know, whatever my wife wants. But I knew what my schedule would look like in the coming years. The job and house and all that would happen in the time frame that it would happen, like it was just a given. Things would probably start coming together by the time I was twenty-three years old or so. Everyone who has a college education immediately gets the job they want, right? That's naive to the *degree of insanity*, but it's the expectations that were built for my generation.

The kids were going to start coming around the time I was twenty-five. This was very deliberate in my head. I wanted enough time to find the right girl, find the right job, and make some great memories before kids. Granted, my idea of making great memories pales in comparison to the crazy adventures that some hope for; I wasn't necessarily looking to party or travel the world, but I did some crazy shit. Okay fine, you've read a lot of the "crazy shit" I did through the course of this book and you know none of it quite reached the same apex as those who have hiked the Appalachian Trail naked or quit school to roadie for their favorite metal band. But you may recall that for an extended period of time, I did eat ice cream and triple berry pie stacked on cheese cake. Show some goddamn respect.

I didn't have any defined goals during this stretch, I just wanted to live a little with no real responsibilities. Once I got tired of that and decided what I wanted next out of life, I would then find a wife. And we would start having kids right on schedule at the age of twenty-five. I'd be old enough to know a thing or two about life, but young enough to be active with my kids and not miss a beat as they moved into their young adult years.

It was a little selfish and presumptuous, but one of my biggest dreams was to teach my sons and daughters the beauty of basketball. And maybe some football, too. I have loved sports for as long as I can remember. It continues to be an obsession of mine to this day. Some of my fondest memories growing up were playing catch with my dad in the yard or shooting hoops with my friends and my cousin. I still play basketball with a group of guys every Thursday night.

Naturally, I would show my kids how to shoot hoops and throw a spiral. We would do this into high school, where I could offer some thoughtful help and encouragement after a rough game or go outside and play a quick game of H-O-R-S-E when they couldn't sleep because of boyfriend problems. We could go to the movies together and eat popcorn while the big screen lit up our imagination. I would show them all of the music that I loved and they would think it was weird the same way I think about my parents' music tastes.

It's become increasingly clear that things never go exactly as you planned. It is 2019, and I am thirty-one years old. My wife and I have been trying to have kids for about six years now. My wife has had to endure a total of six miscarriages, including three during the lengthy course of writing this book. There seems to be no sign in sight of our dream coming true.

I wish I could sit here and pretend that it doesn't matter. For some people, having kids may not be a priority; hell, maybe it's the last thing on earth you would want. That's perfectly acceptable. It's not for everyone. It's always been important to me, though. I think there's sometimes a weird stigma (or conversely sometimes a fetish) around guys wanting to be dads. But really, it's just a normal thing that many of us feel and there's no shame around anyone's parental preference.

Yep, so I'm just a dude that really wants to be a dad. I don't want to be an average dad or *just* a dad. My heart beats to be the best damn dad I could ever be. I've always had this concept in my head that each generation should be better than its predecessor. I wanted to accomplish more than my parents. And I wanted to raise my kids so they could accomplish much more than I could ever hope to achieve.

I'm not sure I have yet accomplished more than my parents, but I always dreamed big. I wanted to be a professional football player when I was eight years old. Around 4th grade, I realized that I was never going to be a very big kid, so football would have to be more of a hobby. So, I shifted gears and decided I wanted to be a Teenage Mutant Ninja Turtle instead. Leonardo was always my favorite. He was a great leader of the squad and had these awesome swords so he was pretty badass. Plus, his eyewear was blue and that was my favorite color. It was an obvious choice for me.

That was the dream. But reality caught up to me there, too. There aren't exactly tryouts for this sort of thing. If football was a long shot, it would seem like being a sewer-dwelling pizza-loving reptile ninja was maybe impossible. Then, I decided I would become a famous rapper. Or become a sports agent. Or write best-selling books (finally, something on the damn list I actually did!).

Despite whatever careers and ambitions I would pursue, that common thread of being a great father was woven through it all. It was perhaps my most important goal outside of being a good husband. I am an intelligent person who is fairly athletic and has a pretty reliable job. That's not exactly the legacy I had hopes of leaving behind. My kids were going to be something else. They were going to accomplish whatever they set out to do. They were going to cure cancer or perform rock songs to sold-out arenas or win an NBA championship. They were going to change the world.

Whatever they would decide to do, I would be so damn proud of them. I would say that out loud and I would tell them that I love them no matter what. And I would ruffle their hair and encouragingly smack their back and show them the proper way to eat tacos. I would teach them how to play video games and properly headbang and where the best seating is at the movie theater. And I would just adore every silly little thing they would do.

Who knew we might never do any of these things, because they might never even get a chance to take a breath?

———————

This whole process is even harder, because my wife has to experience it, too. Dannika is the woman of my dreams. She is an amazing lady, the strongest woman I've ever met. The things that she has had to overcome are both heartbreaking and inspiring. She's also someone who seems like she was born to be a mother.

I don't mean that in the sense that most Christians usually mean. Many Christians act like a woman isn't totally fulfilled until she has children. Like you haven't fulfilled your womanly destiny God has for you until you get pregnant and spit out a baby, at which point you may now be considered on par with the other adults in the room. That is such bullshit.

If you're a woman and you do want to have kids, that's perfect. If you're a woman and you do *not* want to have kids, that is equally perfect. If you don't want to have kids now and someday change your mind, also perfect. You are God's creation no matter your perspective on motherhood and your value is not tied to it. The concept of motherhood being tied to a woman's value is a black mark on the Christian communities that propagate it and it has no standing in truth.

That being said, Dannika is a woman who seemed destined to be a mom. The way she lights up when holding a friend's baby is amazing. The way she can "parent" kids she nannies without even fully trying is nothing short of talent. She can comfort a baby and stop a crying fit that I had assumed would last forever. I've heard people refer to her as the "Baby Whisperer", and it's just true. Some people have a knack for cooking or singing or fixing cars. She has a knack for taking care of kids. It's amazing.

When she talks about her childhood, some of her fondest memories are of carrying around a doll and pretending it was her baby. I don't know, maybe that's typical of a lot of young girls. But it was something different for Dannika. It was a milestone she wanted to experience and live through.

She once *volunteered* to be a chaperone for middle school summer camp. Let me restate: she willingly gave up a free week of her summer to care for other people's children when she had no obligation to do so, because that's what she does when it comes to caring for kids. They were in desperate need at the last minute and she just jumped right in. She came back with all these stories about how she saw these girls experience real life-change and how she wanted to get more involved. She didn't toot her own horn, but I know that my wife helped make those moments of growth and transformation happen.

Dannika has been a nanny off and on since we've been married. There was a little girl she watched for two years, and when the family moved away, she literally cried. She misses that little girl still today. That little girl has a great mother, but she has a woman here in Colorado who loves her in such a motherly way, too. And now she's nannying a pair of siblings that she continues to love on and dote and showcase love to every chance she gets.

And yet, it hasn't magically fixed the hardships that have afflicted us through this journey. I've had to watch as she has repeatedly gone through the hope of that rare pregnancy amidst infertility that has only led to miscarriage after miscarriage. It hurts—what more is there to say? I wouldn't wish it upon anyone. But of all people, I don't understand why Dannika has to go through it. If she could trade our house, the little savings we have, and our cars for her to give birth to her baby, she would do it in a heartbeat. But it's just not that simple.

I wish I could say that I felt no shame in the midst of these trials, but I'd be lying. When this all started back in 2012, I was clueless to the depth that this pain would be felt. My wife's first miscarriage happened prior to us being together. I wasn't there for the hurt, so I won't go into detail. But I know that one of the earliest moments Dannika fell in love with me was when I didn't shy away from her lingering pain. Instead, I told her that I would care about that lost child as if he were one of my own.

I meant it, but didn't know what that entailed, to be honest. I was sincere, but had no understanding of the depth of suffering that goes along with something I had never experienced. The only frame of reference I had was in considering my mom's miscarriage when I was a toddler. I didn't have any memory of it and didn't even know that it had happened until I was an adult. As far as I could tell, while it was a sad thing that she had experienced, it seemed like it maybe wasn't that big of a deal. Obviously, I was just interpreting the data I had, but I didn't consider the fact that I heard about it for the first time nearly two decades after it happened. All that to say, I was upset for my wife but couldn't really understand what she was feeling.

How do you know what true hunger feels like unless you have gone days without eating? How do you relate to someone who is on the verge of starvation? They can describe the pangs that sharply bite into their bloated stomachs, the feeling of lethargy that comes from an acute lack of calories. I can feel compassion. And sadness. But I don't feel that hunger unless I've lived it. And I had never lived anything like this.

When we experienced our first joint miscarriage, Dannika was on birth control. We didn't want the year-long honeymoon to be interrupted by a screaming baby and we were told birth control was the most effective way to avoid any unexpected pregnancies. Truthfully, it wasn't just wanting the first couple years of marriage to ourselves; we were not in a place to be ready for a baby and we knew it. If it would have happened, we would have matured as fast as needed to figure it out. But the plan was to wait a few years and *then* have kids.

Instead, only a couple months after our wedding, my wife started bleeding. Not the normal, scheduled bleeding. It was unusual. It was scary. I don't remember much about it, but we had our first miscarriage together. If I didn't think I was ready for a baby, I promise you I was nowhere near ready to help Dannika through such a tragic loss. It was an immensely sad time, figuring out how to make sure my young wife was physically okay and how to tell our parents.

As upsetting as it all was, a part of me was ready in a couple short days to move forward and not put any more thought into it. I still didn't fully understand the pain that Dannika felt. It just didn't register. I was sad, but even more so I was oblivious. To me, it was a big deal the way that a car accident with an overnight hospital stay is a big deal. It sucked and there would be scars, but eventually it would be mostly forgotten. It would not be a memory that haunts you for years to come.

I tried to be there for Dannika emotionally, but I didn't know how. I know that she would tell you right now that I did a good job, but I still feel shame because I felt so little torment next to hers. I hate to write this, but if I'm being honest, I probably felt a little bit of relief. It seemed like this miscarriage would be easier to overcome than an unexpected child. It was painful, but it wouldn't change the whole trajectory of my life—that was my thought.

Fast forward a couple years. As mentioned above, we had been trying to get pregnant for several years in hopes of a healthy pregnancy all the way through. We finally did become pregnant after three years of trying. It was like a storybook. We were on vacation when we found out. Had we been a little further along, we would have had a chance to tell my grandparents in person that they could expect another great-grandchild. Little did I know that this would be the last time I would see my Grandpa, which would have made it that much more special despite the sad irony.

It was a little too early, though. We wanted to make sure that it wasn't a false positive test and that everything was healthy, so we waited until we got home. A couple days later, Dannika started feeling sick in an all too familiar way. This was the miscarriage that made it finally click. We had been trying for so long, holding out hope for this dream of ours.

This miscarriage felt different. It wasn't an inconvenience, or a scary accident that ended up not being too severe. It was the loss of a child as far as I could understand. And it shed light on the previous ones, too. More than a loss; it was the death of a dream.

———

There's another weird component to this, too. Struggling with infertility really works you over when it comes to your outlook on other people. My wife and I have a lot of friends that we have accumulated over the years. Add in social media, and it is impossible to avoid the countless pregnancy announcements or frequent posts about that adorable thing your kid has done. Johnny is the best at counting and has such a funny sense of humor and the doctor says he is in the ninetieth percentile in his age group: We fucking get it, he's adorable.

Sarcasm aside, we really do get it. We would do the same thing with our kids if we had these moments to tell the world about. It's a constant reminder that our reality doesn't align with our dreams. And it continues to be something that we wrestle with day in and day out.

All right, let's sit here for a moment. If you're pregnant, you should feel free to celebrate it. If your kid took her first steps, make a big deal about it if you want. Not only do I want you to celebrate, but I bet that most people in your life want you to, even if they are going through the hell of infertility. That's not the point at all.

Being pregnant and being parents is hard enough without worrying about every little thing. A measure of tact is always well appreciated, but we are sympathetic to the fact that your life is just as complicated as our own even if it is in different ways.

No, my only point is that it defies reason for those of us who have been trying for years and so and so got pregnant after trying for a few months. Or didn't try at all. Or didn't even want to get pregnant in the first place. Thoughts start running through your head like, "Why the hell would somebody who doesn't even want to get pregnant get pregnant before we do? How does that make any damn sense at all! Why are there people in the world that rape children and literally throw them away and we haven't been able to have one healthy child?"

There isn't a nice, clean answer. It's just a reality that shows how fucked up the world is from beginning to end. I don't say that with humor or sarcasm. I say it as someone who has had his heart broken and had too many nights holding his wife as she cried herself to sleep. It all cultivates a sense of shame from envy and jealousy.

There's also this weird shame with family. My wife and I are both the eldest children in our respective families. We were also the first ones to get married on both sides. And there's this weird pressure for grandkids. Nothing has been overtly stated by any of them, and they are all super supportive and caring for us through this process. But we feel it and think it. We want kids for our own reasons, but we also want kids for our parents. We want them to be able to move into their next stage of life as grandparents and it sometimes feels as if we are holding them back.

And now we have siblings that are married. We want them all to have kids if and when they hope to. We will be happy for them and will celebrate with them. It will be a great day, but it will be a weird day, too. In fact, Dannika's brother and sister-in-law recently told us they were pregnant. And we've had several very close friends all get pregnant around the same time. They all told us so graciously and with heightened sensitivity. And sad though we are that we have not had these experiences, we are genuinely filled with joy for them all. By the time you are reading this book, Dannika and I will be uncle and aunt to a tiny little baby. Because life is too short to cling to what could have been, what will be is that I will be the best damn uncle I can.

This healthier perspective does absolve me from the shame. But it does not erase the anger I still feel. There have been long stretches where I can feel nothing but anger at God. It doesn't make sense that he would allow such things. It's not my constant state as I've grown to view God as having very little to do with the deaths of my babies, but sometimes blind emotion takes me back to that place of rage. That is okay. You can trust God and respect him and still get pissed off sometimes. God is big enough to handle our human emotions. Hell, He created those emotions, right?

———————

Dannika's story is my story, too. Our stories are uniquely intertwined and dependent on each other. That's the only thing that makes sense through this whole ordeal. The tragedy that we have experienced has actually genuinely strengthened our marriage. Howard Schultz said, "In times of adversity and change, we really discover who we are and what we're made of." Dannika and I have discovered that the love and grace we hold for each other has deeper depths than we ever could have imagined.

There still are really tough seasons where it seems a little hopeless. Fighting is eminent. Why don't we do this or do that? There's this new diet I heard about. Try this new supplement. Adoption maybe? In vitro fertilization? Surrogacy? It's all damn expensive, but maybe we would be parents then? Should we just accept that we will never be parents and move on?

Fortunately, we've known from the beginning that we are on the same side and fighting for the same things. If I had to go through these things alone, I can't imagine how I would have survived. There are days where I don't think I can go on, but Dannika picks me up. There are days where Dannika leans into me and tells me that she needs me. And in those days, I do whatever I can to be there for her.

Hopefully someday there will be more than just the two of us. We have a cat. Two cats, in fact. And in some perfectly illogical way, that really helps a lot, despite not currently having kids. Sometimes it feels funny when we are telling people stories of our cats as if they are our children. We talk about how one of them is always grumpy to other people but unrelentingly clingy to us and the other thinks he's a puppy and proves it by eating all human food in sight. I'm sure people think it's a little goofy and incomparable to their children. Ah well, it's a small blessing in the midst of the hell we are going through, and we can only embrace what we have.

But if I am being honest, it's also not everything I have ever wanted.

Saving Grace

Many times, I consider myself a really shitty Christian. Some of you reading this have probably also come to the same conclusion (except you would say crappy because you are closer to sanctification than me). I've certainly given you more than enough detail to consider me as such. When I say I am a bad Christian, I don't mean that I am a bad person or someone God has a problem with. I know I am doing my best to follow God. Rather, we are all bad Christians in comparison to the facade that church culture puts on all of us to be perfect and hide our sins.

When I was a teenager, I started to see through that facade a little bit. There was a time in my life where I refused to sing worship songs at church. That's not entirely true. I would respectfully stand up like everyone else and I didn't make a show out of it. I just wouldn't sing a word that I didn't mean or believe. Not a horrible practice in principle, but there wasn't much coming out of my mouth with all the words about God being great and Jesus saving all. I couldn't find it in me to sing when I felt nothing.

I guess you could argue that it's better not to pretend than to just do it to blend in. Sounds a lot like peer pressure, after all. Others have told me that you should fake it 'til you make it. I don't have any idea what the right answer is. Probably both are just fine under the right circumstances and really horrible under the wrong ones. I find myself singing a lot more words these days.

But some of these songs are crazy in what they are saying and requiring. I was in church just a few weeks back. I was already halfway through writing this book and was pretty well convinced that everything I would be writing about would be about my past. And then my worship pastor pulls this dick move and starts singing "I Surrender All." The lyrics are fairly self-explanatory. There's a lot of repeating "I surrender all... all to Jesus I surrender" over and over again. It's a bit repetitive, but it has a way of lulling you into it until you really ponder what you're saying. I was very familiar with the song and felt it was a solid if unspectacular selection for service that morning. But as I was singing it, I came to an unexpected realization: I have probably been singing these exact words in various church services for 15 years or more.

There was something beautiful and familiar about that. It felt comfortable and warm and... *damn*. There was my epiphany. I had been saying these words for 15 years and had to start wondering how sincere I meant them despite my filter of only singing what I believe. I hadn't surrendered everything to Jesus. Not even close.

Marriage is hard when you're struggling with infertility. Truthfully, marriage is difficult under any circumstances. My marriage is the one area of my life in which my limitations seem to be constantly magnified. They say that marriage is one of the most effective ways by which God will sanctify you. As the church is subject to Jesus, so do you become subject to your spouse. It's an uncomfortable, self-sacrificing status that creates a bond that cannot be replicated in casual relationships.

However, I would also never suggest that you need to be married to have a complete or fulfilled life. Paul literally says it is better to not be married and suggests you should only get married if you can't keep it in your pants (1 Corinthians 8:7, possibly paraphrased). It seems like there isn't much of a biblical basis for marriage being a necessity to happiness. Nonetheless, it's something that has absolutely added to my life. But it's not all roses and candlelit dinners and sex on demand. It's not a dream world, no matter how great it can be.

Case in point, I fight with my wife. At times, we have argued a lot. We are seven years into our marriage and there are some arguments that don't seem to be going anywhere. The worst part is that many times they are over the stupidest things. We have arguments over things like how the laundry is done or why there are dirty dishes sitting in the sink or whose turn it is to clean the litter box. Most of the time, these arguments fizzle out as someone takes the high ground, but sometimes it gets heated and neither of us feel like backing down would be acceptable.

Just to be clear, I am not that guy who thinks that women belong in the kitchen and bedroom. At this point, the whole "shut up and make a sandwich for me or I'll backhand you" joke isn't just not funny, it's really disturbing. Women deserve more respect than that. They deserve an equal partnership, which is sometimes hard to define. In our household, we currently have an arrangement where I work full-time so my wife can work part-time in the nanny role she loves. Given the discrepancy in hours worked, she has agreed to pick up the load of being the primary house caretaker.

Re: primary. As in, not the only one. I am not a misogynistic douchebag. I would go so far as to consider myself a feminist or near to, though they haven't given me my laminated card yet so I could be wrong. I am a douchebag, however, for being selfish and controlling. And picking the worst times to express the way I am feeling. And saying it in accusatory ways. Or evasive, passive ways. Things like, "*We* need to do a better job with these dishes" in which the subtext is, "Isn't this kinda your job?"

When I say that I see no end in sight, I don't fully mean that. As I am writing this right now, we haven't fought about this stuff or anything else in several weeks. It is embarrassing enough to say that aloud (or write it down). I am committed to loving my wife the way she deserves and overcoming my own selfishness and sinful nature. It sounds pretentious when I say it that way, but I really mean it. It is my intention to not have these stupid-ass arguments that I instigate. Rather, I want to show a greater patience, find new ways to show her I love her, and empower her to do the things that are important to her.

———————

This makes me think of another story involving my wife. She's not perfect, by the way. I don't want to be that guy that pretends that his wife and marriage are pristine and without fault (I guess I have already proven that one to be false!). She's stubborn and argumentative and aggressive when she knows she's right. I don't dare continue that list, but you get my point.

She also is an extremely compassionate person and her heart is especially for those who are most on the fringe—the ones abused and neglected by society. Think orphans, sex slaves, and minorities. And homeless people. She's the type to give any homeless person she sees a couple bucks if she has it on her. There's a whole critique on if that is the most effective way to help people in those circumstances, but set that aside for now. The reason she does it is because she genuinely cares. And she will think about that person for days and feel worry for their circumstances.

There was a day when she was at a conference on the other side of town, being hosted at a hotel. There was a woman in the lobby who was down on her luck. Dannika spoke with this woman for several minutes to understand why she was so upset. The woman couldn't afford a room to stay in for the night. Something was stopping her from contacting her family or anyone to come help her. She had a bus ticket to leave the next day but tonight was the problem. She was not super clear on why she was in this predicament, only that there was no solution that she could find.

After talking with her, Dannika offered to help by lending the woman her phone for a quick call, buying her some food to hold her over, etc. All of it was declined, as there was only one thing the woman needed: a room to stay in at this hotel. Dannika spoke with the man at the counter and purchased the woman a room with her debit card. Seemed like the right thing to do at the time.

When I found out that evening, I was livid. How could you do this without consulting me? Why didn't you use an ATM and buy the room with cash instead of our debit card? What if this woman stays several nights charging the card on file? Dannika told me she tried using cash, but the hotel had a policy where they required a card. She took the fail-safe action of having the hotel staff make a note on the account that nothing be charged to the room. That new bit of information did little to change my perspective. I couldn't believe she would just do this without talking to me first. I didn't see it in the heat of the moment, but I was being condescending and rude and an all-around dick.

Some of my feelings were completely fair and legitimate concerns over the method by which Dannika helped this woman. There was certainly a better way to go about it to avoid getting scammed. And I was proven right. The woman ended up opening a tab at the hotel bar and racked up a solid bill that was, of course, charged to the room. Turns out she liked expensive mixed drinks and steak. I was justified in my feelings. I should have said, "I told you so." But I couldn't.

Even though I was right, I knew I was actually wrong. I treated my wife terribly before anything bad had happened. She was trying to treat this person the way Jesus would have treated her. Maybe he would have Jedi-mind tricked the hotel to accept cash or maybe he would have told the woman to go to Pueblo, for there will be a room there. That's a Colorado-joke. Jesus would never send anyone to Pueblo, that is where Hades is. Whatever Jesus would do for this woman, it is clear Dannika's heart was imitating him when mine was not.

Everybody likes to pretend their marriage is without fault. It's one reason why you see so many posts on Facebook that say nothing other than to imply that so-and-so has a perfect spouse, perfect kids, and a perfect job. There's certainly also some decorum and social rules that govern it inappropriate to air dirty laundry online. That's probably healthy to a degree, but it sure as hell isn't healthy to just pretend everything is perfection.

Josh Roggie

Imagine if every movie followed a flawless hero who never made a wrong decision and only had to overcome slightly inconvenient things that happened to them, in the end finding blissful happiness. Sure, there's nothing wrong with seeing such a film once in a while. But at some point, it doesn't just become boring; realization dawns that it is disingenuous and meaningless. Life hurts more than that and it gets uglier than that.

At one point, my best friend Jon lived with Dannika and I for a stretch. It was a mutually beneficial arrangement where he could help us out with the bills while living somewhere much cheaper than getting a place to himself. Overall it was win-win. But there was one time where Dannika and I got in a heated argument with Jon in the room, and I would be a bonafide liar if I didn't include it in a chapter on our marriage. It was one of those throw down, knock-out fights that just isn't going to end with a panel decision. Someone's going to metaphorically get knocked on their ass with blood dripping from all the wounds on their face. Both sides are going to be hurting after.

As is typical with many fights that go that way, it started with all three of us (Jon included) debating somewhat congenially... about artistic integrity, of all things. My memory of it is fuzzy, but at some point, it went sideways and Dannika and I made it pretty personal. It went from a spirited debate to raised voices and Jon trying to surreptitiously absorb himself into the couch.

One thing to know about Jon is that he is never afraid of a good ol' fashioned debate, no matter how contentious it gets. I think arguing may be his love language. The way I understand it, he basically calls his mom a couple times a week to argue and debate about politics, theology, etc., and they spend hours doing it. And he never seems to be mad when he gets off the phone. It seems like it energizes him and makes his day better.

So, you know this must have been an ugly fight for him to bow out. It might be the worst fight Dannika and I have ever had. It is without a doubt the worst one anybody else has ever witnessed firsthand. It ended with me literally yelling at Dannika, her yelling right back, and me raising a white flag in a quiet, fragile voice before walking outside and sitting there for an hour with tears in my eyes.

I've never asked what happened next from Dannika's perspective. I would bet she went quietly upstairs and had her own tear-filled alone time. I'm sure Jon just sat on that couch for 30 minutes to let all the tension cool off. He finally came out to me and we talked a bit and I didn't say much because I was not only ashamed by what had happened but also by the fact that he had been there when it had happened. Eventually we went inside. Jon probably played some X-Box. I talked to Dannika and we both apologized. That was a few years ago now, but it still sticks in my head. My marriage couldn't be portrayed as perfect to my best friend. He saw one of the ugliest moments.

We still argue, but it rarely gets in the same zip code as that fight. That was one for the ages and hopefully we will never get to that level again. As embarrassing as it was that Jon was there, it seems like the best part of the fight actually was that someone observed it. It made me realize how obsessed with being right I can be, to the detriment of saying sorry when I know I should. It feels more right to dig in and entrench yourself instead of looking for a way to meet in the middle.

Simply put, I need to increase my grace for my wife. Which brings me back to that damn song about surrendering it all. How can I have so little grace for my wife? This is the one person on earth that I love more than any other. She is the most important person in the world to me. Not only that, but she is also the only person in the world that I have offered solemn vows to. I haven't made a promise like that to anyone else, ever. And the heart of those vows is to put her first and to care for her as she does the same for me. She is the one that I have promised to be with through sickness and in health. She is the one who has worked with me through infertility and a painful sexual history and nearly everything else you have read about in this book.

And yet, I don't have enough grace to treat her the way she deserves one hundred percent of the time! So, what makes me think I deserve so much more grace than this from God? In truth, I know I *don't* deserve it. To deserve something is to show qualities worthy of earning such a reward. My actions would indicate that I don't deserve unending grace by any logical standard. I sing these words to God about surrendering all and making him my king and how wondrous he is and all of these things. But if you look at my life as a whole, those words seem to be hollow. I have done plenty in my life knowing damn well that I was doing it for me and in defiance of Him.

I guess my saving grace is that my wife still loves me. She tells me that daily and doesn't hold it against me when I don't treat her fairly or when I am overly critical or especially rude. She doesn't leave me and find someone better, even though she probably could. Her actions repeatedly emphasize to me that she loves me unconditionally. She is the most clear demonstration of God's unconditional love in my life. If my wife can have that much grace for me, how much more graceful can God be?

XII

D is for Depression

"I Never Got to See the West Coast" by Emery

The church teaches a lot of things about sex. Interestingly enough, very few of these so-called teachings are said and most of them are actually implied. Sex is only for married people. Sex is only for a man and a woman. Being a virgin is the most important thing you can give to your future spouse. Many churches have an underlying theme that sex is only for procreation. Any lingering thoughts on someone's hot body is a sin of lust. And once you lose your virginity then you can no longer provide the most valuable gift possible to your future spouse.

Then there are the justifications and interpretations that are layered into the conversation. Making out is probably okay, unless it gets too steamy. Cuddling is okay and wandering hands can be okay so long as it doesn't lead to sex. Sex is anything with the word sex in it (oral, anal, etc.). Or maybe anything that involves penetration. Or maybe everything is okay as long as it isn't a penis in a vagina. Looking is okay, touching is not; thinking about it is a gray area. And the list goes on and on.

I don't have all the answers, but I know all of this was confusing as a teenager growing up and trying to toe the line between controlling my hormones and maintaining purity. It seemed like the rules were all different depending on what adult you asked, but nobody was brave enough to encourage me to be mature and learn what was safe and acceptable for me. Everybody wants there to be well-defined guidelines, but it doesn't work if there isn't a consensus (or if the consensus is utterly unrealistic).

When I was a twenty-something who had sex with a kinda-sorta girlfriend who was simultaneously estranged from her husband, I knew I was fucked. I had nothing to offer any other woman and had no way of recovering any semblance of purity. The only thing I could do to fix this was to make it work with that specific girl. She had my virginity, she had my love, and she now had my future.

The problem was that she wasn't taking my phone calls and she was actively ignoring my texts. I don't really know why. Maybe she was embarrassed. Maybe she felt pity for me. Maybe she was genuinely as confused as me. Maybe she was mad at me for making it into such a big deal. But I just had to talk with her. I decided the only way to make this happen was to go to her in person where she couldn't avoid me.

I didn't like the idea of confronting her outside her home, especially since she may have still had a boyfriend and I knew I didn't want him to see me there. It seemed like my best opportunity would be her work. She was a caretaker for a family about 20 minutes east of Colorado Springs, in an area called

Black Forest. It's a geographically large area with expensive homes spread out over thousands of acres. I didn't know the address, I only knew one of the main roads that led there. So I did the only logical thing I could come up with. I drove most of the route to Black Forest and parked my car on the side of the road. It was a warm spring afternoon, and I was a desperate, lost man.

After sitting there for a few minutes, I realized that the cars were driving by pretty fast and she may pass me before noticing my car parked on the side of the road. I got out of my car, climbed up the trunk, and sat on the top of it. Looking back at town, Pikes Peak towered over the city in all its snowcapped glory. Clouds started to shroud the edges of the mountain range, but the peak stood there like a sentinel unmoving from its post regardless of the circumstances. I stared at it, believing that if I could be as unfaltering as that mountain that she would have to love me and be with me.

I sat there for two full hours, not quite knowing the exact time she would be driving home. I talked to myself, rehearsing what I would say. I mumbled some prayers to God, unsure if they were being heard or just bouncing off the clouds and falling back to me. I cried and used my sleeve to wipe those tears when the occasional good Samaritan passerby would stop and ask if I needed some help with my car.

She never came, or at least I never saw her. My prayers fell on deaf ears. I got into the car and started to drive back. A deluge of rain and hail started slamming into the roof of my car. It was the loudest noise I've ever heard in a car. I couldn't even hear my music at full volume. There was no distraction other than the adverse weather. I was left alone with my thoughts. My eyes started to mist again. And for the first time in my life, I wondered what it would be like to actually kill myself.

———————————

When I'm driving in a winding mountain pass that has deep caverns and suspect railing, I sometimes wonder what it would be like to spin the wheel and go crashing off the road. When I am going 70 mph down a two-lane highway and see an 18-wheeler truck coming at me, I wonder what it would be like to swerve right into their oncoming lights. One reason I don't like heights is because when I am looking over the edge at a hundred-foot drop, a part of me can't help but wonder what it would be like to jump off.

These are not the thoughts I was thinking in that car. These are morbid curiosities. These are wonderings of the adrenaline rush and sheer chaos that reflects what stunt doubles do for movies. These are the musings of the carnage that would result and how awesome it would be playing out on a big screen.

No, I am saying that while I was sitting in the car on a rainy night that I thought that the world would be a better place without me. There was something wrong with me, likely something incurable, and a mutual separation would be best. I was broken and my future was already in jeopardy, so what harm would there be in shutting it all down? People would be less stressed, happier, and generally uncaring in regard to my absence.

I think the only reason I didn't do it was because I didn't want to upset my friends and family. They would probably be happier in the long run, but they would cry a lot of tears between now and then. They may even blame themselves, despite it not being their fault at all. I was also only kinda unsure about what God thought about people who committed suicide. I grew up being taught that murder made someone hell-bound and suicide was a form of murder without a chance of repentance. I don't believe that at all now. God certainly has enough grace and mercy for someone who feels like they can't keep living with their afflictions. But at the time, it was a thought that circled in my head. Finally, a small part of me was still repackaging my delusions of reconciliation as optimism: I wanted to believe this could still all work out with Sara.

I felt this way every day for weeks on end. I couldn't tell you how long it lasted. Time is not a real thing in seasons like this, it is only a construct that is shrouded in the pain. I found myself drowning in this head space day after day after day. And then one day, there was a brief reprieve and I felt balanced and normal again. The next day the gloom came back in full force. But I would occasionally find reprieve and eventually those moments of reprieve became more and more frequent.

Once it started to fade, I began to realize that this wasn't the first time I struggled with anxiety, depression, and the loss of peace when these feelings overlapped each other. As you may recall, I was not exactly the most popular kid in school. That was a constant until high school. Though I was not the most popular kid in high school, things did start to change for the better. I went to a small, private school my sophomore year and really felt like I fit in from day one. The school was set to have its first Homecoming that year and I somehow convinced all of my classmates through a joke to vote for me for Homecoming King. Considering I was in the largest class in the school at that time, I won. Things appeared to be looking up.

But you read the chapter where I got bullied and beat up and very nearly swirlied a good many times. Somewhere in there, I lost my confidence and was bitten by the anxiety bug. It's not that hard to figure out some of the baggage. You get beat up and picked on often enough, you're going to start wondering what you can do to avoid it. I tried dressing cooler. I tried to talk the slang a little bit more. I tried being better at sports. I got picked on for my knock-off brand clothes that couldn't quite replicate the fashion of the expensive, name brand ones. I didn't know the slang and made myself look like a fool. I actually was decent at sports, but it didn't make a damned bit of difference. Every day was a new adventure. What will I get picked on about today? But it wasn't just that.

The anxiety permeated everything. When my parents were separated, I was constantly concerned about them getting back together. I would sometimes wonder what I could do to make it happen, not knowing that there was nothing I could have done. When they were back together, I shifted the anxiety to my school work. I was a sharp kid who always got good grades, but I felt no sense of accomplishment. I needed perfect grades. Math and English came naturally and were not a struggle, but Science was a whole other story.

In 4th grade, we started exploring the basics of chemistry. At one point, it involved us lighting a match. The teacher was going over and over the fire safety rules and how to be really careful. I must have been daydreaming or became too bored with waiting, because I stopped waiting and just lit my match. Apparently, we were still doing test runs (how many damn test runs do you need for lighting a match!), because I was the only one to light it. I stood still in a bit of a stupor as one of my classmates pointed this out and everyone began to laugh a little. The match was burning down and the teacher ran over and knocked it out of my grip, rushed me to the sink in the back of the classroom, and started checking my skin for burns and washing my hands.

There were no burns, but I felt the pain of embarrassment and shame. Come on, that could have easily been a prank or intentional disobedience for the sake of humor, but it wasn't. I couldn't feel like I was being funny, because I was too worried I might be in trouble. Some things like this seem inconsequential and silly, but there must be a reason I still remember it twenty years later, right?

That same year, we had a science project where we had to make a visual representation of a specific flower, with each of us getting a different assignment. It was considered a major project. Let's face it, a "major project" in 4th grade isn't exactly weighed as heavily as a major project in college. But I was convinced this was make or break, fail and repeat the class next year territory. I was assigned the Carnation.

I never much enjoyed any projects like this and was super stressed about it. I hated anything that allowed creative freedom, because I wanted rigid rules to know exactly how to game the system and get that A+ I needed. But this assignment did not provide that level of specificity. I thought I would try to be creative by using a model car with tons of country flags and banners sticking to it; get it: a car made up of nations. But doubt nagged at me. What if this isn't what the teacher meant? What if my play off a pun crashed and burned? What if they were expecting me to draw a diagram illustrating what makes a carnation a carnation and not a rose? Am I sure carnation was even the flower assigned to me?

I was so upset the night before, I remember being in bed and literally sobbing. I didn't typically cry, because it led to more bullying. You had to be tough. I remember a bully once telling me after he hit me that men don't cry. We were 9 years old and he was trying to avoid discipline. I don't think he meant much by it and more likely an older sibling or tormentor said the same thing to him at some point. I get it and I forgive him. And I have long since un-learned that ridiculous perspective.

But that night I was crying and didn't care if men should cry or not. My mom came in to check on me and was shocked to see me so upset. She did what good Mom's do and helped me calm down. She looked at my project and told me how impressive it was and that it would definitely get a very good grade. And she told me that she was happy with me no matter what grade I got as long as I could tell her I did my best.

I'm not sure I fully believed her, but I did eventually fell asleep. And everything went well from there. Interestingly enough, I don't remember what grade I got. It was at least passing as they did in fact let me move on to 5th grade the following year. But I still hadn't shaken this sense of inferiority. To this day I still tell people that science has always been my worst subject. There's really no evidence for this. I've gotten A's in every science class I have ever taken and I've read several lengthy well-respected science-based books by the likes of Jared Diamond and Bill Bryson and others. And yet, my mind was set at that young age: I am terrible at science and always will be.

Upstate New York gets very hot in the summer, at least by my standards. Between the beating sun and the high humidity, it was unbearable. I found myself playing outside nearly every day in the summer of 1996, trying to beat the heat at the ripe old age of eight. We were limited to how much "screen time" we got, so my siblings and I were ushered outside daily. We were absolutely content with that. With an overactive imagination, there was no limit to what could be found outside. We had a huge rock formation behind our house that was a "fort," and we had sticks for swords and would be transported into other worlds. We had a basketball hoop and a cheap above-ground pool, and a swing set. We were not wealthy, but you run out of excuses for boredom pretty quickly with options like these.

The imagination is an odd thing. When you are that young, you really buy into your thoughts. It all feels real. Dreams feel real, too. And nightmares. Imagination is not purely a good thing.

On one of those hot summer days, I was outside by myself and parched. As far as I was concerned, I may have been dying of thirst. Whatever game I was playing couldn't wait for me to go inside and get a drink. I needed relief right now. I noticed that next to the house there was a plastic bottle filled to the brim. It was a big one, the 64 oz type. The same type that juice comes in, except for the label had been peeled off. The golden, rich liquid in it looked like delicious apple juice.

The thought of that smooth, sugary drink running down my throat triggered the same brain nerves as ecstasy (probably). I opened the lid and proceeded to take a huge gulp of it. Something in me stopped it at one swallow. A bitter taste filled my mouth and my brain tried to compute what had just happened.

The smooth consistency of the liquid coated my throat. It was warm from sitting in the hot sun. It burned weird when I swallowed the one gulp that I had braved. I believe it was gasoline for a lawnmower though I honestly never found out. My parents had a habit of repurposing used bottles to save money

Shame

and not be wasteful. It didn't take me long to realize this liquid was not a beverage to drink. And it certainly wasn't apple juice.

I don't remember much because my mind jumped to the only logical conclusion: I had just poisoned myself and I was going to fucking die. I was paralyzed with fear. It seems like there is an obvious solution here. Tell my parents, figure out what the liquid actually was, they make me throw up if it is toxic, tell me everything is going to be okay, etc.

I just couldn't tell them. I pretended it never happened and I didn't tell my siblings, either. It was not just embarrassing, it was frightening. And I couldn't show my fear. Fear is how you get beat up at school. Fear is how you prove yourself unworthy of being a man. I wanted to prove that I was worthy. So, I made the only logical conclusion: I am either going to overcome this, or I am going to die trying.

Hours went by and nothing seemed to happen. I didn't do much more playing (what game would be satisfactory for your last hours on earth?), but I also felt more or less fine outside of my thoughts. I wasn't vomiting or exhibiting any other symptoms that they list on poison control warning labels. Maybe a slight stomach ache, but nothing worse than any other time I have felt extreme anxiety. Eventually, my concern passed as uneventfully as the rest of my day. I was alive, but I could have actually died if I had drunk a more damaging chemical and I had accepted that possibility. Looking back, it appears safe to say that I had issues even as a child.

According to the Anxiety and Depression Association of America, over 16 million adults experienced a major depressive episode in 2015. It appears as if that number has likely continued each year since, if not increased. Keep in mind, that is only considering people 18 years of age and older and there is no doubt that children and youth also suffer from depression. Anxiety disorders are much higher yet, affecting 40 million adults a year—which is approximately 18% of the adult population.[1] Depression and anxiety are pervasive disorders that haunt large swaths of society and it feels as if we are only now touching the tip of the iceberg when it comes to learning how to talk about it. For my part, I find that my mind is most settled and at peace when I read someone else's story and all I can think is "me too."

I had mentioned that in high school I had won Homecoming King. That is completely true. And it should have been an incredible night where I was thankful for being well liked and appreciate the people around me. Hell, I should have at least enjoyed it on equal grounds with any other high school dance. These are supposed to be fun nights, after all. But that night was absolutely miserable for me.

I was still very self-conscious about my teeth, so nearly every picture from that night shows me smiling tight-lipped to hide my mouth. There was no way in hell people were going to see how big my teeth were. I didn't have the courage to ask a girl to the dance, because I was worried she would say no. I was the Homecoming Fucking King and still had no confidence. So, I was there alone, watching the girl I actually had a crush on dancing with other boys.

I also didn't even participate in a single dance, because I couldn't get myself to ask any girls to dance (see above) and didn't want to make a fool of myself on one of the group dances

---

1   https://adaa.org

like the Electric Slide. Not only was I scared of being rejected, but I was also scared a girl might say yes! I had never even slow danced before and was sweating buckets at the thought. It was horrible. I almost would rather have not gone at all. I hadn't gone out to dinner with a group beforehand and I left the party all alone. I was probably the loneliest Homecoming "King" in the history of the tradition.

The following year, I was on the basketball team. I would not call myself a superstar and wasn't team captain, but I contributed skillfully off the bench. And I was anxious before every single game. I don't mean anxious the way people get butterflies in their stomach and need to listen to loud music to get into a zone. No, I was in a bathroom stall dry heaving and having diarrhea. Every. Single. Game.

It is normal for teenagers to be uncertain about themselves and feel nerves around public events, but (most of) my teammates didn't have these types of reactions. As an adult, I feel much more self-assured, but these types of feelings still afflict me. Recently, my church had an event where we meet up with homeless people downtown and find out what would be on their Christmas wish list. After hearing their stories and hearing what they would want, we would go to a store and buy the things, wrap them, and bring the presents back later in the day with food.

It's a beautiful thing and sounds a lot like the teaching of Jesus. The problem was that I didn't want to do it. That's not precisely true. I knew that I definitely *did* want to do it, and I knew it was valuable and meaningful. I was chosen as one of the leaders to help organize it, as well as help in a small role with the service the night before. Yet, my stomach was in knots that entire week leading up to the event. I felt so anxious about going so far out of my comfort zone and speaking with people who deserved this. They don't have a choice in being outside of their comfort zone. They sleep outside in the cold some nights and go days without eating. They just want someone to help them without coercing them or raping them in the middle of the night, which is a story several of them had experienced from people pretending to be good Samaritans. It is disturbing how many of the *haves* take such advantage of the *have nots*.

Leading up to the event, I wondered if I could get sick in a way that people would believe instead of thinking that I was lazy or uninterested in helping. I pondered who I could delegate my tasks to so I wouldn't have to do them. Dannika knew I was more anxious than sick, but also knew that those two can many times be the same thing and didn't pressure me into going despite wanting me there. I knew she would be willing to "cover" for me.

None of that happened. Instead, I went and had a Godly experience in which I saw the Christ. I met Christ in an awesome guy named Jerome who desperately wanted mittens. He is a homeless gentlemen who no doubt had a needs list a mile long, but he was so adamant that a warm pair of mittens was all he really wanted. I was dying laughing as he outlined an argument worthy of a dissertation to why mittens are far superior to gloves for keeping warm when you are stuck outside in the coldest stretches. Though it was absolutely funny, it was also a moment that cuts to the heart. There was something truly special about Jerome. I don't know a single thing about what he believes, but I swear to God there was something of Jesus in his eyes.

Finally, we left the park and went shopping. We probably could have gotten a pair of mittens at Wal-Mart for eight bucks and rushed back and he would have been deeply thankful. But Jerome deserved the best we could manage. We drove across town and went to REI and bought a heavy-duty pair of moisture resistance ones that would keep his hands both warm and dry. When we returned to the park, we had only one person present the gift to him because we didn't want him to feel like it was a spectacle about us. I subbed in for someone working the food truck so I didn't get to see how he reacted when he opened the present. Part way through my food serving shift, he popped his head in the window of the food truck and was yelling boisterously about these amazing mittens he had just gotten. His eyes were lit up like a Christmas tree. I am not exaggerating when I say that the only time someone has ever reacted that joyfully to a gift I had given them was when I proposed to my wife. He was absolutely thrilled. That's the true spirit of Christmas, Charlie Brown.

Anxiety is a bitch. It keeps me up at night. It tells me that I was made for something more than this, but I will never be able to accomplish those things. I will always be what I am now. It makes me think that I should not share my thoughts and concepts such as those in this very book, because it is all useless drivel and meaningless. And it threatens to cause me to miss moments with people like Jerome that have the power to change my life forever.

———

There's also a special high when it is overcome. I knew I wanted to marry Dannika, but our wedding day was one of the most anxious days of my life. At one point, I was at the front of the room and about to walk onto stage with our officiant. I made a mistake in having all my groomsmen and my best man on the other side of the church, because they were going to walk their bridesmaids down the aisle before my soon-to-be wife.

All morning, we were in a back room to ensure that I didn't see the bride before our vows. We had food in there, but I couldn't eat anything. The service was around noon and I hadn't eaten any-thing all day. The little bit that was in my stomach was skipping rope every which way. I lucked out, though. Matt Codd had made the trip despite having not seen me for a couple years. He also happened to be one of our officiants and was the one who would introduce me and get the party started. He cracked some jokes backstage with me about how the ceremony is nerve wracking, but what I should actually be nervous about is the late-night hotel room activities that would take place later. Matt's always been like a big brother so he also had a calming presence as he talked about how awesome marriage was and he would know since he had already been married for a few years now. Of course, it would all come at a price. Later in his speech, he alluded to my high school dreams of rapping and people calling me J-Ro and a number of other mildly embarrassing stories. But there was no mention about my almost bathroom mishap in a minivan in Wyoming while his twin tortured me, so there is that.

The moment had passed and we were walking into the sanc-tuary and standing at the front of the room. I don't remember much else. Only my best man escorting the Maid of Honor, giving me a goofy thumbs-up and exaggerated smile. And my incredible bride being led down the aisle with the most beauti-ful tears in her eyes. Everything else about that day was just an amazing blur. I suppose that's why you invite the most impor-tant people in your life to be in your wedding party: getting married isn't something you can do alone.

One more note on anxiety. There are only a couple chapters left in this book and anxiety somehow made its presence at the end, despite it being obvious that it's something that has been sprinkled throughout my whole life.

The deeper I got into this project, the more I learned an obvious lesson: writing a book is hard. This is my first real attempt and the closest I have gotten to finishing it. I had some great momentum early on and carried it into the middle portion once it had been fleshed out and well-outlined. Then I hit the proverbial wall that everyone talks about. Can confirm, it's a real thing. And I didn't write again for weeks. I couldn't convince myself to do some editing. I didn't even stare at the screen for hours on end, knowingly lying to myself that I would find my rhythm any moment now. I couldn't muster anything to move forward.

Every time I thought about this project, I thought about the ways it would fail and prove to be meaningless. I thought about how I will have wasted several years of my life bleeding onto pages that nobody would feel worth their time to bother reading. Little did I know, it would also take me more than an additional year after writing the last word to be brave enough to send a proposal to a publisher.

It's no coincidence that I hit my tallest, hardest of walls when I knew the chapter on anxiety and depression was the next one I had to write. This chapter is not the one with the most shameful stories and considering the statistics of depression, I know I am not alone. However, it felt like one of the most personal because I STILL STRUGGLE. The things that trigger my anxiety and depression have evolved as I've aged, but they're still ever present. I hope to someday be free of this thorn in my side, but I've accepted that the only thing I can do right now is say "Fuck it" and take one more step forward.

XIII

An Exercise in Futility

"First Father" by Silent Planet

A lot of these chapters have been about the pain and shame that people have caused me. People are hurtful, sometimes even when they don't mean to be. I can attest to that, since much of the content in this little public journal also involves me shaming and hurting others.

But the further I dug into the shame I have felt, the more I came across yet another unexpected source of shame and guilt that was weighing on me. I started to realize that I also felt shame over my theology and the ways I viewed God. For example, even the language I use for God is flawed and in need of repair. And no, I still don't think He gives a fuck when I swear; He is more concerned with what I mean and feel in my heart whenever I communicate. I'm referring to the ways in which I have viewed God as a clearly defined, black and white figure.

It all started with my views on the Bible. The way I was raised was very much a "God said it, I believe it" perspective. This is a common phrase in Christianity and many people still take this approach. It really only works if you view the Bible as infallible, inerrant, and uniquely inspired by God. Using those beliefs as a foundation, you can then believe the Bible is filled with the literal words of God that people just transcribed.

This view worked for me through my formative years, because I was willing to take it at face value. It was during the hardest stretches of life that these beliefs were challenged. It started with my relationship with Sara and the fallout of it crumbling. I was taught that reading The Bible would be a comfort for the hardest times, but I found no solace in it. The relevant passages that I knew were judgmental and only contributed to my hopelessness. Granted, there are scriptures that maybe could have helped me, but I was never taught how to dig for them. All of my lessons involved "sword drills" where an instructor called out a passage and whoever found it and read it first won the game.

I gave up on the Bible for some time. After all of the things with Sara, I was in a college class focused on the Bible and there was a bonus assignment to read the entire book through the course of the semester. I had never read the Bible from beginning to end and it seemed like an interesting challenge. So, I read it in the span of four months. It was eye opening to read it for myself and see the ways in which the passages in the Bible didn't align with how these stories were applied in so many sermons I had heard. For example, I had heard so many sermons on how the focal point was that Jonah had been swallowed by a literal whale no matter what science suggested and so few sermons on how God was teaching Jonah a lesson on loving people who he considered his mortal enemy.

I started actually studying the Bible and found there was a wide range of interpretations of numerous Bible scriptures and I could no longer look at it as purely black and white. That led me to the realization that I had to adjust my views of God in the same way. For so long, I had been taught that God was a "He" pronoun, because that's typically the way the Bible phrases it. However, the Bible is not consistent as it uses female metaphors for God, as well. There are passages where God is described as a mother hen sheltering her offspring under her wings (Matthew 23:37). Isaiah 66:13 says, "As a mother comforts her child, so I will comfort you; you shall be comforted in Jerusalem."

I needed to reevaluate how I saw God. God is not a God-like version of a man. I still use the He-pronoun out of habit (that also probably needs to be reviewed), but I believe God is every bit female as male. God has no genitalia to biologically define a gender and is the Creator of both genders who were made in God's image. I grew up in a world that wanted clear definitions for God, but I began to realize that there was a greater mystery at play. We use language to try to communicate what God is, but it is merely metaphoric and analogous and will never fully capture God as He is too vast. And as I began to realize that God was different than how I was raised, it was revealed to me that I needed to question the ways in which I communicated with Her.

Prayer has always been a confusing thing to me. At its simplest, I was taught to talk to God the same way I would talk to a friend. Adults would tell me that it is all about building a relationship. Imagine a conversation you would have with a close friend or someone you are becoming quick friends with. Emulate that.

"Hey God, I really think the Lakers have a chance at the NBA Finals this year. You think they have it in them?" "Dude, God, that brunette girl in Creative Writing—I think her name is Dannika—she's super hot, right? Seriously, you should see if she likes me." "God, I would love to be a NY Times' Bestselling author. That would be amazing. Could you buy a few copies of my book in support of my dream."

If that sounds weird to you, it does to me, too. Especially, because I'm not just talking to my best friend about what's on my mind, I'm talking to the SUPREME OVERLORD OF ALL CREATION. It always seemed kinda trivial to tell the MOST HIGH BEING all these meaningless little details. Add into the mix that God knows everything and is omniscient and it makes even less sense. The only logical thing to do is talk about things that really matter. And since you're supposed to talk to God every day, you find that you're repeating yourself a lot.

Add in that you live in America and have most all of your primary needs met and God quickly turns into Santa Claus. What the hell, sounds reasonable to me. The Bible even says ask and you shall receive (Matthew 7:7). Says so a couple times, even saying that you will get it if you believe (Matthew 21:22).

I don't think it was immature of me to start praying that God would make pretty girls like me and make tests go well and that I would get a good job and so on. I wasn't necessarily always selfish about it, either. Sometimes I would pray that famous people I looked up to would become Christians. I once prayed every night for months on end that Eminem would become a Christian. It would have been amazing for him and would have been a huge victory to the glory of God if he were to convert.

Imagine the dopest rapper lacing his songs with lyrics about how God saved his life.

There's nothing wrong with that. I think most people probably pray that way. But I noticed something. Eminem never got saved and released a dope gospel record. I was never very popular with girls. My life is not perfect. My wife and I still haven't had children. In summary, it hasn't made a damn bit of difference.

I don't feel shame over asking God for peace in the midst of pain and I don't even feel shame over voicing our hearts' desire that my wife and I have children. If you are praying to God about something important, please continue to do so. But know that it may not happen, whatever you want. It may happen later or the opposite may happen or nothing at all may happen. That isn't an indicator that there's something wrong with you.

Even so, I was ashamed that I had treated prayer like a gum ball machine, where I put in a quarter and expect a treat in return. Those work every time. Sure, occasionally you've gotta shake it a little or get an attendant to help, but you always walk away with a gum ball. Prayer is not an "input required article and receive desired output" tool.

It's not just me whose prayers go unanswered, either. I have friends who have lost parents to illness despite them praying for weeks on end. I know people still afflicted by their mental health despite pleading to God that they be healed. I've read the stories of refugees in other countries praying to God for rescue even as bombs continue to blow up their friends and family. I was treating prayer like the gum ball machine and that only leads to one conclusion: God is not as good as me since I would cure, heal, rescue. I didn't believe that God is not good, however. So, I had to be wrong about God's character or about prayer. I chose the latter.

I am still struggling with prayer and the purpose it holds. I've come to believe it is somewhat similar to meditation. I've found quiet moments of thinking about nothing and being present make me feel closer to God. And in clearing my mind, I believe that God bubbles to the surface the thoughts that need addressing. I don't know if I would relate it to a relationship like I have with my friends who reside in the physical realm; I think it just might be better to find that quiet, calm place where God feels inside of you. *Finding God in the Waves* by Mike McHargue was a very helpful resource.

I have also found new meaning in public prayer. Many times, public prayer is used in the form of petitioning. You might pray before an event with the people working it. Or you might pray at a funeral or in a church service. Many people use this moment to ask God to be present or to move in the hearts of those attending or to place peace on the minds of everyone in the room. Considering God is always present and always moving towards open hearts and bringing peace, you might consider this repetitious. I disagree and would still encourage those prayers to be said. I'm not convinced that prayer changes what events will come, but prayers like this can change the mindsets of those hearing them and can ultimately have the desired effect for peace, spiritual awareness, etc.

If my perspectives on God's identity and prayer needed to be reshaped, then what of baptism and spiritual warfare? Many denominations believe baptism is a requirement to be saved by the grace of God; turning down the opportunity for this declaration is akin to saying that God is not a priority.

There are certainly deep-seated arguments that debate if baptism is required or not, as well as debates on what methods are valid forms of baptism. The way I look at it, God in his infinite grace is trying to find every way possible to justify saving someone and bringing them closer to Him. I just don't see a gracious reasoning to conclude that your heart was in the right place, but you didn't get submerged or sprinkled or do it publicly instead of privately so you are doomed.

I can't say I have always felt that way. I was about 10 or 12 when I got baptized. Myself and a couple buddies, including my brother, all got baptized on the same night. Our church required you to meet with the pastor in advance and explain why you were ready. That was a bit intimidating, but we had a nice pastor that didn't pressure you into anything, so it wasn't as traumatic as others may have experienced. My parents talked to us after about how serious this was and it wasn't something to do just because your friends are doing it.

They were doing a pulse check to make sure it was something I was ready to do. Of course I was ready! I was 10 years old. That's gotta be right around the time of the age of accountability! If you're not familiar with that phrase, it's a concept that our church had that stated if a child died before coming of age, they would be bound for heaven. But once they hit a certain undefined age of maturity, they would be considered an adult in the eyes of God and old enough to have made their decision. It does seem important enough to have a specific age in mind, but it seems as if nobody can agree on this and it's more of an estimation. So, 10-year-old me thought that if I died in a car accident or a bus ride or falling out of a tree, I would be the dumbass who went to eternal damnation because he didn't swim at church.

I didn't say that to my parents. Why would I? That's why everybody gets baptized, isn't it? If it is needed to avoid burning in hell forever, then just do it. I was very serious and sober and got baptized. But something weird happened. I didn't really feel any different. I thought for sure I was supposed to be like a new person, but I felt exactly the same.

It all happened on a Sunday night, during the summer so there was no school the next day. A large portion of the church met at a campground outside of town. The church met at this campground a couple times every summer for various outings, and it was always fun. I was hopeful we would roast hot dogs and marshmallows like we usually did.

We were all to be baptized in Black River, which runs through the area. It gets its name from being so murky. I didn't want to be in it very long, because I have an unfounded fear of swimming in water that is not clear. Anything could be in there, ready to bite off my toes or other extremely important and sensitive appendages. The water in upstate New York is cold year-round, so it was freezing to be standing in it despite it being a hot July day. I was shaking as I stood in knee-deep water waiting for my turn.

One of my friends went first. The pastor said the dedication about baptizing him "in the name of the Father, Son and Holy Spirit" and dunked him under water. My buddy leapt out of the water after coming up and acted like he was stepping off stage after an encore performance in front of a sold-out arena. He was throwing up peace signs and whooping. I thought it was an interesting blend of funny and uncomfortable, because it seemed like this should be such a somber event. Like walking to the gallows and getting diverted at the last second.

Finally, it was my turn. So I walked out, got dunked, and was baptized. That's all. I'm not entirely sure what I was expecting, but I didn't feel a sudden reassurance descend on me or a form of empowerment or anything. I just felt even colder since I was now wet from head to toe. I shivered as I walked up the embankment to my parents, who were holding a towel and change of clothes for me.

The rest of the night was a lot of fun like all of the other summer outings. I did indeed eat some hotdogs grilled over a fire pit. My friends and I played football until it got too dark. We never did get to the marshmallows as a rain storm suddenly moved in. There was distant thunder booming, warning us all to take cover. We packed everything up and headed home. It was one of the loudest storms I can recall. It was even scarier because we were outside in the middle of nowhere and driving home.

My mom said that it was Satan showing his displeasure, because my brother and I were baptized and our baptism declared that we belonged to God. I've never had a serious conversation with her about this so I'm not sure if she actually believed it to be spiritual warfare or if she was just trying to comfort the three scared kids she had in the back seat. It was a little confusing, because she used to tell us when we were younger that thunder was just God playing bowling. Maybe there are multiple causes for thunderstorms.

At any rate, I still didn't feel any power or any real difference. I was ashamed, because I wondered if this meant that I wasn't really saved because I didn't really believe. It seemed like there should be some proof or guarantee that the ritual was performed correctly. I wondered if I should get baptized again, maybe when I was a little older or meant it more than I did that night. But then if I said I needed to be baptized again, it would feel like I was insincere the first time. It seemed like a trap either way.

I followed a similar path with baptism as with prayer. I do not at all believe baptism affects your status of salvation, but I would encourage people to do it if it will bring them closer to God. It never did that for me. I was using it as an insurance policy to make sure my eternal destination was locked in. The curtain in my mind has since been torn and I now see that it is not a machine where following a certain subset of rules is designed to create a precise outcome.

This sounds depressing as hell. You're telling me that if I follow all the rules and do everything I was told to do that my life won't be any better? What if I go to church every Sunday, even though football is on? What if I show up again on Sunday night and Wednesday night and Saturday morning? And if I don't smoke, drink, or chew or go with girls who do? And I stop hanging out with my non-Christian friends because they will drag me down?

I'll be saved then, right? When I discovered that these changes may not even make my life any better and have no real guarantees of salvation, I was shook. All of Christianity started to feel like a con. And that's when I started to really believe in God. The further I removed myself from the cycles of shame and guilt and obsession with proper theology, the more I was able to see and feel God.

At one point, I would have told you I was a sinner. I have done hateful things towards individuals and sometimes even whole people groups. I didn't follow the rulebook: I had premarital sex, I masturbated, I lied about people and laughed at them and mocked them. I have become so angry that I have said very hurtful things to people I love.

And I will continue to make mistakes like these that show that I am not ready to live up to the standard of uninhibited life that I was designed for. I will also continue to have blindspots revealed to me that will require changes to my perspective and my lifestyle. I welcome those changes as that is the way to continue to move toward peace for mankind.

But I have found that becoming a Christian isn't about a checklist of things you no longer do. And it's not about saying a specific prayer that only works if you say the exact right phrases. It's not about getting baptized, because you've been told that holy water prevents hellish fire. It's not about defining God so perfectly that the mystery is squelched.

It's about putting yourself in places to see the Christ. It's about finding a quiet space free of distraction and seeing what God places into your mind. It's about talking to hurting people and just listening and all people are hurting in some way so be free to show no discrimination in who you spend time with. See their humanity and Jesus will show you his divinity.

Jesus was God, but he was also a servant. Serve people. You need food? Let me feed you. You need water? Clothes? Have my jacket and let me get you something to drink. You need someone to tell you that you have value? I have a friend who tells everyone he has a heart to heart with that they are the light of the world. He is right. You are the light of the world.

Throw away the game. The bubble gum machine is designed to keep things simple, but ultimately it is an unsatisfying answer to a beautiful mystery. Discard it. Use prayer and meditation and baptism and any other sacrament that you would like to continue to dig further into the mystery of the universe. May each layer bring a fresh awakening in your life.

XIV

God is Where You Look

"In Between" by Beartooth

When I was growing up, we went to church a lot. We were one of those families that was there Sunday morning, Sunday night, and Wednesday night. When there was an open gym night on Friday, we were there. In hindsight, it probably wasn't like that every single week of every single year of my life. But it felt damn near close.

Tack onto that the Vacation Bible School at my church and the programs at other churches nearby, too. Add in events like potlucks where everyone brings a plate of food to share and Super Bowl celebrations and "Harvest Festivals" (because Halloween is evil but a party on the same night with free candy and games is okay under a different name). Let's not forget summer camp and community outreach fairs and the list goes on and on.

I enjoyed a lot of these things. I also spent a lot of them sitting in my parents' car flipping through my football cards, wheeling and dealing with my best friends while the grown-ups did their thing. And yes, I was still listening to really shitty Christian music very loudly. One time, I messed up the speakers in my parents' car by listening to Michael W. Smith. This was not exactly earth-shattering rock music.

As I grew older, I stopped caring altogether about the church portion of church functions. By the time I was in youth group, it's fair to say I was there just for the fun games and the girls. That's what happens when there are literally jokes going around among the adult leaders that it's best to have hot girls in your youth group to keep the guys interested. Isn't that absolutely crazy? But it's also completely true. Sex sells, so why wouldn't the youth pastor use the "Jesus version" of a Carl's Jr. ad?

Needless to say, I didn't feel a whole lot of God in what I was seeing and experiencing in church. And to be fair, I wasn't even really looking for God. I was just looking for fun. But the church should have pointed me to God and let me decide if I wanted to be a part of it or not. I also don't think the churches I went to were especially at fault, so much as the whole system was in the crapper. If I went to another church across town, I was just as likely to encounter the same feelings and same tactics.

That got me thinking. Like I said, there was some serious systemic issues at play here. But was that all there was to it? Could I just blame it on the Church as a whole or was there something else at play? I've heard a saying before: "Run into an asshole in the morning, you met an asshole. Run into them all day and you're the asshole." I guess the common denominator throughout all of these experiences was... me.

————

One of my biggest complaints with church is how boring and uninteresting it can be. When you go to church as often as I have for 20-plus years, you start to hear the same sermons. You know you can check out around Memorial Day and Fourth of July and Christmas and Christmas Eve. Mother's Day and Father's Day are both bullshit, because there is no Children's Day sermon. And don't get me started on election season sermons. I've heard pastors make the totally ungodly decision to push for candidates by name despite their history of warmongering or financial corruption to benefit their partners or a whole string of other immoral behavior, all because said candidate was running under the pastor's beloved political party.

I went to church out of obligation. And it was a bag of mixed results. I would feel bored and disinterested most Sundays. And then there was the absolutely abhorrent worship music. As I was growing up, I came to realize that church music was just bad. Sometimes you would have a stirring moment where the Holy Spirit overcame the awfulness or there would be a special from someone who should clearly be the one *always* holding the microphone, although if you go to a church that does "specials" then you know this is unlikely.

I'd be a hypocrite to say I have always felt this way. There have been times where I did feel a little something of Jesus, even in the music. Those times were usually when I could focus enough to ignore everyone around me and be in my own God-zone.

There were other times when watching other people worship would make it feel more real and tangible. And still other times where watching people felt like a trigger for a re-evaluation of if this whole thing deserves cult status.

But my God, does the church ever suck at respecting the arts! We learn in history that most of the greatest artists, especially in the Renaissance period, had patrons from within the church. It's one of the reasons why so many classic paintings and sculptures are of biblical figures and events (things like the naked David statue and that naked man floating on a cloud painted on a ceiling—huh, it's weird how much nudity there is in Christian art).

Somewhere along the way, the Church forgot the value of art and storytelling and musicianship. We gave up excellence for function and affordability. I'm not saying to throw money at the problem. But how interesting would it be if churches started film schools and music classes and writing groups? Imagine if they encouraged artistry and excellence and let God handle the theology behind each piece.

It would be even better for the church to really lean into artistic integrity and allow for the art to speak for itself. No need for an altar call at the end of the song or a dramatic moment where the main character finds out that he is going to hell because he didn't say a specific sequence of words. It's really embarrassing, if we're being honest. And even the little bit of effort that is put into the arts is often more exploitative than anything.

I remember a Halloween one year growing up in New York. We went to a church in a town nearby and attended an event they had that was a drama about salvation and hell. These types of events are usually under the name "Heaven's Gates, Hell's Flames." It's essentially a play where several different skits all have the same theme. A teenager gets drunk and drives into a tree, killing him and his riders. A forlorn woman has an abortion. A man is greedy and cracks jokes about stealing from his company while sleeping with his secretary. Every scene ends as these demons that (in hindsight) look to be dressed in poorly rendered Darth Maul costumes come onstage and drag the sinners to hell while rock music plays and strobe lights go off and the victims let out blood-curdling screams.

It's shitty acting, shitty theology, and all-around bullshit. I remember being a 10-year-old boy thinking to myself that I was really screwed because I had said some bad words the week before or was mean to my little sister or played a violent video game with my cousin. What if we had an accident on the way home and I died and went straight to hell? It's moments like this that perpetuated the fear that inspired my baptism.

The more I experienced these types of sleight of hand parlor tricks instead of perpetuating the teachings of Jesus, the more disenfranchised I felt. I felt like I was an outsider who didn't belong there any longer. Even worse, I felt outside of what the world had to offer, too. Remember how I experienced bullying, long-desired relationships that never formed, and an uncertainty of what my future should look like? Not wholly unique things to feel, but it definitely led to me feeling like I didn't have a home and I didn't belong. I knew I wanted "to belong" with God, but His place was church and I was an outsider. Until I realized that you can't be outside of God, because God is everywhere.

———————

Pantheism is the belief that God is everything. I don't accept that. I am sitting in my chair in my office while typing on my computer. Though I am thankful for each of those things, I don't believe they are God and thus worthy of worship or adoration. Rather, I believe God is *in* everything. While my computer is not a god, it is a result of God. God creates the universe and humanity, humanity designs a tool, and the tool is a reflection of its creator.

This mindset allows one to see God in all sorts of unexpected places. For each person, individual tastes and interests will attune them to find God differently. Some may find the holy moments that I have experienced to be familiar, while others may consider those very same moments profane and false. But all truth belongs to God so I try to open my soul's eyes to see Her in every moment.

One way that I find God is through nature. I think many people can relate to this. Most people have some level of appreciation for rainbows and sunsets and mountaintop scenes where you can see green valleys stretching for miles. I live in Colorado Springs and am thankful to be surrounded by beauty. I love hiking and placing myself into nature rather than just looking at photographs. The city hugs up against Pikes Peak and there are hundreds of trails within an hour or two from my home.

There's something about being away from all the technology and sound pollution and concrete that makes the Holy more apparent. I don't go hiking by myself most of the time. I am usually with a friend or two. When we are in the city, we typically watch TV and play video games, but hiking releases us from these distractions. On our hikes, we end up having deep and provocative conversations about politics and sociology and books we are reading. These are holy moments, even through the times when God is not explicitly mentioned. This is community.

I have been on these types of hikes with people who are not Christians, too. I have found that we have the same types of conversations even if we don't believe the same and I feel God's presence in those differences, as well. Talking with someone about the things they feel and think and believe reveals God in them even if they wouldn't use the same language. There is no us and them, we are all on the same journey and God will be revealed to everyone.

However, Christians sometimes say absurd things about being in nature. They say something like "you can't look at a sunset and tell me that God doesn't exist." They used to say that about rainbows before the gays stole them. Rainbows are still beautiful and even more so when they symbolize someone showing the world that they are now willing to openly accept themselves. But as beautiful as rainbows and sunsets are, they do not prove God's existence. It takes only a basic understanding of science to understand why there is a sunset. And I personally have felt something special and indescribable when looking at a sunset. Maybe it was God; I would say it probably was. But that doesn't mean it is proof of anything other than the rotation of the earth.

It degrades both God and the beauty of nature to try to make a sunset an argument for God's existence. Just be present and enjoy it and feel whatever feelings you feel.

Stopping all the distractions and being quiet and listening is what allows God to effervesce to the forefront of our minds. Another great opportunity to listen to people is found when you serve others. There's a reason Jesus demonstrated servitude so much in the Gospels. It puts yourself into a place of humility and moves someone to a place of acknowledgment and favored existence. It is an exchange of genuine love with no strings attached.

I had experienced a special moment of servitude when I was in youth group (see, it wasn't all bad). A handful of us who were tagged as leaders within the group went out to a park at two in the morning. Despite later getting thrashed by my parents for being out so late, I fondly remember that night. Our youth pastor had pulled out some water and a bowl and towel. We all sat in a circle and went around washing the feet of people that we had personally offended or needed forgiveness from. I was still quite new to the group and did not wash anyone's feet out of anxiety and discomfort. I wish I had, but this did allow me to observe the beauty that was happening. Teenagers were washing each other's feet and apologizing for very specific ways in which they hurt each other. Tears were streaming down everyone's faces and there was so much peace in this park. I wasn't sure that something like that could be done authentically on a corporate level, but it was that night.

I have fed the homeless a few times and volunteered at soup kitchens and gone to an old folks' home and sang (terrible, off-key) Christmas carols. I felt God at all of these things. I am not tooting my own horn, you have likely done this as many times or more. This is how you will feel God. I wanted to feel God in church, but I had forgotten that God is felt in serving others.

To feel God in nature and in serving others is likely not shocking to anyone. Jesus himself seemed to have done both of these methods on many occasions including isolating himself in the desert for 40 days and washing his disciple's feet. But sometimes it's hard to go hiking or to hunt out an opportunity to spend several hours serving others. It can take a lot of energy and sometimes I want to be lazy or only do something fun. Fortunately, God is in everything and moves in those moments, too.

Have you ever watched a basketball game where the team is just clicking? Maybe you couldn't give a shit about sports—that's okay. But there's something really special about a team that moves in rhythm and is all on the same page and successfully pursuing their end goal as one unit. This makes me think of the so called "Hamptons Five" lineup of the 2017 Golden State Warriors. Funny name aside, their style of basketball was so fluid and team-centric that they could go against any opponent's game plan and win. They never lost a championship when they were all healthy, though they eventually disbanded. It was not only talent, though they had that in abundance, but it was also the willingness to sacrifice individually to play their best.

I won't wax poetic too much on this, but I feel God when I play basketball. There's something about the grace and creativity of the sport. There are some rules to create an expectation on what is allowed, but there's a lot of subjectivity that allows for an innumerable amount of actions that could happen on any given play. It's an incredible feeling to have a great defensive play or to score an unlikely layup with the defense draped all over you. Or to complete a perfect pass through a tiny hole that only you and your receiving teammate really saw from beginning to end.

Not all games are like this, but it is euphoric when you get even the slightest taste of the level of basketball that the "Hamptons Five" play. When you get into the rhythm of the game, you stop consciously thinking. Your body is just moving and doing. At the risk of overstating it, it seems as if a level of meditation is accomplished. I feel God in that. Everything outside of the boundary lines blurs and mutes and becomes nothing. It's just me and nine other people in a small, rectangular space with one goal.

I guess this could be accomplished in most physical tasks. If you're really good at meditation, you could probably achieve it without any physical behavior to distract your ever-moving mind. I'm not that way. I'm not practiced. I need a physical distraction to settle my mind so I can just be.

Another distraction that has this positive effect for me is rock music. Like, really loud in your face rock music. And fast and heavy and violent. There's something visceral and real about much of the music that I listen to that I can't seem to find in pop music. Listen to whatever you want to, but find something genuine and meaningful. For me, I've had so many memories where God has shown up in a mosh pit.

Beartooth is a band that comes to mind. I saw them at a small, grimy little venue in Colorado Springs called The Black Sheep. I've been told it used to be a strip club, so it's not exactly the cleanest place. But it is an awesome stage to see a band on. It's tiny and loud and in your face. You are a part of the crowd no matter where you stand.

Beartooth played there in Fall 2014. I was on the edge of the mosh pit, jumping around and screaming along at the top of my lungs. I looked at the faces in the crowd with me and noticed that there were a couple hundred other people doing the same thing. This band has songs about overcoming parental violence and alcoholism and depression and many other curses. Some of the lines were screamed defiantly, as they were my plight. I realized that the ones that were not relevant to my own pain were still being screamed for those around me. My parents have never beaten me, but I guarantee you some of the people in that room had to deal with that demon in their house. We were screaming these lines together because we were on the same side.

"Do you feel strong ruining the lives of everyone you love?" "Listen to the sounds of your children revolting!" For one night, we stood together. These are the types of places to feel God, even with people who don't know how they feel about God.

Recently, I saw Silent Planet perform at that same venue. This band is very special to me. They seem to believe many of the same things as I do and their lyrics challenge me to further understand my assumptions about complex issues. They also are not rock stars—they are down-to-earth, normal guys that care about people in every city they play in. After every show, the singer waits to meet anyone who wants to meet him and a line develops shortly thereafter. The venue keeps playing loud music over the speakers as everyone cleans up, but he waits to talk to each person.

Dannika and I had met him once before and I knew I wanted to once again. The first time, I felt too self-conscious to say anything. I didn't want to lose my chance this time. A small thing I noticed while we waited our turn. Every time he was done talking to someone, he would proactively move towards the line to the next person. Even his body language demonstrated how much he cared for these strangers who relied on his music. When it was my turn, I had to shout over the house music. I told him how hard faith had been lately and how it seemed so overwhelming. He gave me the most genuine, tight hug and whispered words of encouragement into my ear. He was Christ holding my broken spirit.

I had another moment along these lines a few years back. I got to see Emery in concert in another small venue, this time in Denver in June of 2017. They have a particularly beautiful song titled, "I Never Got to See the West Coast".

I would say I am a fairly emotional person, but rarely do I allow my emotions to be visible. I hide them inside and process them where it is safe. But something about that night hit me in the strangest of ways. That song is about someone who wants to commit suicide being pleasantly surprised when they tell someone and find that the other person has felt similar things. They find comfort in not being alone. Emery played that song and I was singing along and tears just streamed down my face, because I knew I was not alone.

———————

Up to this point, it basically sounds like I am saying church blows and is a waste of time. I'm not *exactly* saying that. But I'm also not NOT saying that. It doesn't make a whole lot of sense to look for something at church that I can readily find elsewhere. I think it is because I have been doing church wrong this whole time. I've gone there looking for someone to give me everything I want.

But when church is done right, it's really a very good thing. Somehow, the American Church has fallen into the trap of wanting to look a certain way and be a way to trick people into wanting to come in and give their money and feel good (or bad, if you're into the hellfire and brimstone) and repeat next week. That's not what the original church was. It wasn't really a place at all. Instead, it was a community. Like at that kick-ass rock show. It's a group of people feeling each other's pain and saying, "I don't know how to fix what you are going through, but I will head bang with you and scream at the top of my lungs."

The early church was a place where nobody wanted anything, because everybody shared whatever they had. They didn't have everything they could ever want, but they knew they wanted to take care of each other rather than spend their lives pursuing materialism or a false sense of power. No, it was a place built on servitude and sacrifice.

A lot of people want to abandon the big lights and silly sermons and stained-glass windows that cost a fortune. I don't think that abandonment is a requirement, though it's absolutely fair to question what needs to be modified. But just like the church needs to be changed, so too does my heart. I am a selfish bastard who doesn't like to share and likes nice things and complains but sometimes has a hard time affecting change. I know my flaws, but even in knowing, I still cannot overcome. And yet, there is enough grace for me.

The Church is home to millions of people like me. It takes time for a course correction. I'm thankful that there is a place for me in this community, even if that place isn't what tradition taught me. Change will require authenticity and honesty across the board. But it can start with one person. That doesn't mean you have to stay in church. I recently left my own church because it no longer felt like church to me. In time, I will find another community that will be my church. I don't know if the building will look the same, in fact I don't know at all what I even want in a church right now. I'm not even sure it will be a church, rather than just being an intentional community.

I do know that churches and communities are both full of people and people are complicated. We cause each other hurt and shame when we don't intend to. The church institution is flawed and deserving of so much critique. And those critiques should continue to be levied at the system that it may grow. Nonetheless, I'm thankful that God has no walls that restrain Him. God is in everything and that includes me.

Epilogue

So there you have it. We have made it through an entire book! I have written my first full book and you have read it. We have explored the nuances of shame, guilt, and embarrassment. Though they are not precisely the same, these feelings tend to interconnect and overlap and they all lead to a common result: they hinder growth and limit your potential. We have studied the effects of shame, as well as the effects of releasing shame, on my own life. And yet, I have a sense of shame even as I write these final pages.

I wanted to write a memoir about myself. Some of my favorite non-fiction books are memoirs. As I was outlining it, I kept feeling that my story was not enough. I've always felt this way. In church, people will sometimes awkwardly ask you to write down your testimony. The idea is that this is your story about how you became a Christian and this is how you will convince other people to become Christians. I've always felt very self-conscious about this. The interesting stories are the ones of people overcoming chronic drug use or tragic violence and pain. The interesting stories have a moment where God spoke to them and the clouds broke and heavenly light shone upon them. I have no such moments.

My story is quite run of the mill, with no extraordinary supernatural climax. I was ashamed of that, degrading myself below more dramatic stories. I came to a revelation, however. There are a lot of people who feel the same way I do, falsely believing they have nothing unique to offer. I wanted to write a book that people would relate to, one that would cause the reader to see images of themselves in the pages. As I realized the ways in which shame has colored my life, I saw the ways in which it influences others, too. We are all human, and as much as our stories are different, shame has at one point or another held us all captive.

I dream to be an author someday. See how I said "someday" there. For some reason, I *still* don't feel like I have made it. It's this ultimate identity, this place I want to be. Not entirely an end goal, but certainly a check point that is still somewhere in front of me. But what will it take for me to see that I already am an author?

It seems like anybody who has written anything essentially has the right to call themselves an author. I have written a book now. Two, in fact. I didn't mention it until now, but I have also written a book of "poetry" that is essentially a collection of emo lyrics that never made it to song. It's called *A Medley of Sleepless Nights* and was only ever available digitally on Amazon. It sold about 10 copies, I think. I'm pretty sure most of my family didn't even bother to read it.

So now I've written an "actual, real" book. It has multiple chapters and more than one hundred pages and thousands of words and even has a table of contents. There is a printed version of it so you can hold it in your hands and read it like a "real" book. I meet the definition, but I still don't identify as an author. Maybe when I'm done writing an actual novel then I'll feel as if I am truly an author? Maybe I will consider myself an author when I can say that it is my profession. Maybe I'll be an author, a true to life, authentic writer of words, when I am getting paid for it and can quit my day job and make writing my career.

I think I am realizing what it will take to not feel shame over the a-word. An author is a writer. I just need to write.

That's it. When I think about how to become a writer, sometimes I think about marketing strategies and books I want to write and what coffee shops will make for the best environment to be productive. I think about what my book cover will look like or what books I need to read beforehand to research and prepare. I think about the content of the book and spend weeks and weeks typing up and editing outline after outline. I take notes late at night when I can't sleep. But I will be damned if I am actually going to sit down and write that damn book. I keep forgetting that authors are writers and writers write.

I have been thinking about getting a tattoo for years now. As you well know by now, I grew up in a very conservative environment and tattoos were definitely viewed as sinful. Of course, I no longer believe that. At the same effect, I'm thirty-one years old and not too interested in doing something just for the sake of rebellion. I need more purpose behind something before I feel compelled to be a rebel.

Even when I was feeling defiantly rebellious, I went and got my ears pierced. Boys weren't allowed to have their ears pierced in the high school I went to, so that was the first thing my buddy and I did after graduating. Still have them in fact; seems to fit with my punk rock tastes. Tattoos fit that paradigm whole-heartedly, too, though. And yet, still no tats.

I'll admit that I am not particularly fond of needles. That's certainly a part of the equation. But it's bullshit if I try to sell you that needles are the biggest reason, so don't buy it. I'm afraid of needles the same way I'm afraid of eating sushi. Millions of people have done it and not died. Most people talk continuously of how obsessed with it they are and how they can't wait for their next delicious sushi dinner. Despite my aversion to seafood, I'm sure I'll try it someday.

No, it's not the needles that bother me, but the commitment. Tattoos are permanent, more or less. Once there, you've got them forever. Do I really want to spend a couple hundred bucks on some designs on my arms that I may not want five years down the road? By the way, it's still there even if you decide you don't want it. And I hear that tattoo removal hurts like a mother, too.

You wouldn't wear the same clothes and designs that you wore five years ago, right? Seems like a reasonable point, but very quickly diminished when I look at my own closet and see t-shirts from my college years. I have basketball shorts that I wore to practice in high school and I still wear whenever I lace up today. I have band t-shirts from several years ago that I cycle through for casual Friday. I still listen to a lot of the music from then and some of my favorite foods have been my favorite since high school. I guess it doesn't hold up that I wouldn't want it later, especially since you can always cover an unwanted tattoo with a new one.

Fair enough, but then there's the whole concern over career and professional interference. I don't want to prematurely disqualify myself from a job, because of my appearance. I've believed that for years now. I know what you're thinking: "Josh, didn't you say you currently work in a call center?" That's true. I work in an environment where I am allowed to wear anything that is not offensive and the definition on that is acceptably loose. Many of my supervisors and leadership have varying degrees of ink.

Let's face it. There are very few professions and industries these days that would have any real reason to discriminate against tattoos, and if we're being honest, we know that it's not really holding anybody back. Even more so, I have no interest in working anywhere that is so stuffy as to not allow a tattoo. In case you haven't noticed, I don't really feel like spending all my fucking time trying to be refined in meaningless, insubstantial ways just because it's the polite thing to do.

The heart of the issue has nothing to do with my external circumstances at all. I still don't plan on getting a tattoo until I know what design I want. But I also don't want to hide behind these other inconsequential reasons, because I am afraid of risking something.

There are a lot of great quotes about risk. Benjamin Franklin said, "nothing ventured, nothing gained." Wayne Gretzky famously said that "you miss 100% of the shots you don't take."

I'm not quite in the same class as a founding father and a legendary hockey player, but I have one, too: "risk is a bitch."

That's why I don't write. It's risky to put yourself out there and it requires aptitude to not embarrass yourself in the process. It takes a lot of time to get good at something, to actually be able to demonstrate a degree of expertise. Malcolm Gladwell popularized a theory in his book, *Outliers*, that proposes that it takes 10,000 hours for someone to become an expert at any one thing.

That's a hell of a lot of time to spend practicing anything. To be fair, I would say most published authors haven't put in that much time. But I have heard that the average author writes six books before getting one published. Of course, technology now allows for anyone to self-publish as I demonstrated with that first poetry book I had released. But even now, overnight success is a rarity. Sudden and rapid ascent almost never happens and is even less likely to be sustained. All I can do is write more words and do so sincerely so that the meaning bleeds through even though I have yet to put my 10,000 hours into the craft.

I don't feel shame over the writing I have done. There are some embarrassing things in this book, but I stand by them. I feel shame over the writing I have *not* done. It would appear that the only thing left to do would be to get off my lazy ass, get over myself, and write. I have found through the process of writing this book that I can do it.

This is not a self-help book, and I would question your current place in life if you think it is. It has done more for me through the process of writing it than I could ever have hoped. My book in and of itself is not capable of changing your life. But releasing the shame that acts as a millstone around your neck will open doors to a new life. You were not meant to be burdened by the guilt you carry. What dream do *you* have that you are afraid to pursue?

Don't ignore what makes your heart beat. One day, you will wake up and realize the American Dream of having a good paying job and a savings account and an expensive house was all a hollow promise filled with emptiness—in this day and age it is a construct to create consumers. Don't hide from yourself. The costume you wear to cover your shame hinders you from knowing your true self. When you come to that realization, you will experience depression and feel emptiness. Maybe even despair. I know you will feel this, because it is what I felt every day of writing this damn book. But it's never too late, for you or for me. Start right now and don't stop. Use your scars to propel you to your new life.

Keep writing.

Keep singing.

Keep building houses.

Keep developing software.

Keep cooking transcendent food.

Keep hoping.

Whatever your dream is, take risks. Nobody has ever looked back at their life and wished that they had pursued their dreams less. There is no shame in taking chances, but I have found shame in fear. I am releasing all of my shame by facing my fears. The words are down on the paper, release them from your heart.

Let shame die.

Acknowledgements

I feel like I should thank every single person who has touched this book and offered feedback, listened to me ramble and mumble my way through a brief description, or even just offered generic encouragement to not give up. It has all meant a lot and encouraged me to get to this place of sharing it with the world.

I would like to thank some people by name. If I have forgotten anyone, that is my error and not an indication of the ways in which you have contributed. My bad.

Thank you to my earliest beta readers: Jordan Andler, Lindsi Miller, and Jonathan Grimo. Special thanks to Champion Beta Reader Adam Brewster, who was extremely thorough with his feedback. Thank you to McKenzie of Gold Raven Editing for helping me clean up my early drafts. Thank you to Matthew Codd for helping me work through some of the actual beliefs that became the book, and for writing the Foreword. A very special thank you to my friend and co-host of The Harbor. podcast, Jeff Mason, for reading an early draft and strongly recommending I send it to the awesome folks at Quoir Publishing. And many thanks to Rafael and the Quoir family for respecting my vision for this book and challenging me to make it better than I ever could have done on my own.

A very special thanks to my family for bearing with me as I bare my soul and for being especially encouraging down the final stretch. And finally, a very special thank you to my awesome wife, Dannika. Thank you for encouraging me to be brave in the midst of sharing the most shameful and embarrassing parts of my life and for being a safe haven when I need refuge from it all.

Thank you, dear Reader. I appreciate you taking the time to read what will likely be the most personal material I ever share. There will be more in the future and it may be poetry or a novel or another memoir or who knows what else. I appreciate your support and hope that you may continue to find your path to freedom.

The Soundtrack

If you weren't paying attention, here are the songs that got me thinking about each chapter. You should absolutely take the time to look up these songs. There are some gems in there. And yes, they are generally of the punk/rock/hardcore persuasion. Many of these artists are my favorites because they write the most sincere, genuine, heartbreaking music I have ever heard. It will be well worth your time looking them up.

1. "God's Gonna Cut You Down" by Johnny Cash
2. "Scissors" by Emery
3. "Seventy Times 7" by Brand New
4. "The Restless" by The Matches
5. "Typical" by MuteMath
6. "Gasoline" by Brand New
7. "Last Chance to Lose Your Keys" by Brand New
8. "The Third Way" by The Classic Crime
9. "Na Na Na" by My Chemical Romance
10. "Slave to Nothing" by Fit For a King
11. "Our World is Grey" by As Cities Burn
12. "The Weight" by Thrice
13. "I Never Got to See the West Coast" by Emery
14. "First Father" by Silent Planet
15. "In Between" by Beartooth
16. "Deathgrip" by Fit For a King

For more information about Josh Roggie
or to contact him for speaking engagements,
please visit *www.facebook.com/joshroggiewriter*

Many voices. One message.

Quoir is a boutique publisher
with a singular message: *Christ is all.*
Venture beyond your boundaries to discover Christ
in ways you never thought possible.

For more information, please visit
www.quoir.com

CPSIA information can be obtained
at www.ICGtesting.com
Printed in the USA
BVHW071952260220
573388BV00004B/399

9 781938 480539